■ ■ ■ ■ ■ ■ DEFEND YOURSELF ■ ■ ■ ■ ■

DEFEND YOURSELF

*The Complete Guide to
Self Defence, Personal Safety and
Security at Home*

ERIC BASKIND

PELHAM BOOKS

PELHAM BOOKS

Published by the Penguin Group
27 Wrights Lane, London W8 5TZ, England
Penguin Books USA Inc., 375 Hudson Street, New York, New York 10014, USA
Penguin Books Australia Ltd, Ringwood, Victoria, Australia
Penguin Books Canada Ltd, 10 Alcorn Avenue, Toronto, Ontario, Canada M4V 3B2
Penguin Books (NZ) Ltd, 182–190 Wairau Road, Auckland 10, New Zealand

Penguin Books Ltd, Registered Offices: Harmondsworth, Middlesex, England

First published in Great Britain 1993

Typeset in 10/12pt Raleigh Medium by
Goodfellow & Egan Ltd, Cambridge
Printed in England by Butler & Tanner, Frome

A CIP catalogue record for this book is available from the British Library
ISBN 0 7207 2027 3

The moral right of the author has been asserted

Contents

■ ■ ■ ■ ■ ■ ■ Foreword ■ ■ ■ ■ ■ ■ ■

Self Defence in this day and age is an emotive subject. Too often we read in the media about instances of intimidation, assault and rape, where the average citizen in the street is the unfortunate victim. A little knowledge of self defence could be enough to prevent you becoming another of these victims.

As a result of the increase in violence, there is a growing interest in self defence and in specialist books describing its skills. So, when choosing a book on self defence, the questions arise, 'What can it do for me?' 'Can I benefit from reading it?' 'Can I put it into practice?'

When I received the manuscript of *Defend Yourself: The Complete Guide to Self Defence, Personal Safety and Security at Home*, I realized that here was a self-defence book that has been specifically written for the average citizen. It has been written in a clear and concise manner, instructions can be followed easily and the skills can be learned easily by observation and a little practice.

Eric Baskind shows his depth of knowledge of all aspects of self defence, from the first awareness of danger to restraining an attacker. In addition, the no-nonsense, practical advice about personal safety ensures that the reader fully understands the principles behind this vital subject and that he can easily put them into practice. This book should be compulsory reading for everyone.

Defend Yourself is a major contribution to self defence and personal safety and I have no hesitation in giving it my unqualified support.

Ross Alexander Jackson
June 1993

Ross Jackson is a serving police officer and was appointed a police physical training instructor in 1984, a position he held for several years. He is also a police self-defence instructor and holds black belts in a number of martial arts systems.

Since Ross Jackson is a serving officer, it must be emphasized that the opinions expressed are his own and do not necessarily reflect the views of the police establishment.

■ ■ ■ ■ ■ ■ Introduction ■ ■ ■ ■ ■ ■

We all know that in recent years there has been an escalation of both violence and crime. Hardly a day goes by without news of an assault or some other type of crime – very often against innocent people quietly going about their normal business. To reduce the danger of being attacked in the street or at home, of being the victim of a crime or simply of being in the wrong place at the wrong time, it is now more important than ever to learn how to protect and defend yourself and your property effectively.

Most people are terrified with the thought of becoming the victim of a crime, especially a violent one. With the help of this book you will be able to replace fear with knowledge, submissiveness with assertiveness, and weakness with competence and self-confidence.

Everyone has the right to feel safe in their own home and on the street, yet in today's society self defence and personal safety have had to become subjects of ever increasing importance. However, much of the available tuitional material falls far short of what is required to enable you, and those with you, to protect yourselves and to deal effectively with any threatening situation with which you may be faced.

This is where this book is different: it is a complete system of self defence, personal safety and security developed for every man, woman and child who wants to learn how to protect and defend themselves effectively and to remain safe. The book also deals with the non-physical aspects of self defence and includes practical ways of avoiding trouble before it starts. In addition, it contains valuable advice about security and safety, covering both the home and when outdoors. The essence of this system is safety. Safety to enable you, and those with you, to go about your everyday lives with the confidence that everyone needs and deserves. By heeding the advice offered in this book, your prospects of being able to avoid becoming a victim are considerably enhanced.

Strength and size are not essential in being able to master the self defence techniques taught in this book. This is simply because those in our society who go about attacking and robbing others, often select people who are considerably smaller and lighter than themselves as their victims, with many of their innocent victims being female.

With this in mind, I have developed this system so that every technique taught can be applied effectively against an assailant who is much bigger, stronger and fitter than his victim.

Knowing that you can defend yourself should it be required will give you added confidence and a greater feeling of security.

(In this book I have referred to the attacker as 'he'. This should be taken to refer to either he or she, depending on the circumstances, and does not imply that *women* are never the aggressors.)

> '*Until I learned how to defend myself, I couldn't have imagined that I would have been able to fight him off. He was so strong. Whether it was the surprise of my resistance or some other reason, I succeeded. He even muttered an apology to me as he ran off.* '

■ ■ ■ ■ ■ The Aims of this Book ■ ■ ■ ■ ■

The prime aim of this book is to give you the ability to be able to go about your everyday life in safety and without fear of attack or falling victim to other types of crime. Whether by giving you the skills needed to deal with a potential threat by non-physical means (which is preferable), by arming you with the technical physical ability to deal competently with actual violence or simply by giving you added confidence, this book will prove to be invaluable. You must never forget, however, that your own safety and security must always remain your principal objectives.

The book also deals extensively with both safety and security and provides, in an easy-to-follow text, straightforward and invaluable advice that will help to protect you, your family, your home and your possessions.

Learning about self defence and personal safety can only enhance the quality of your life.

Men, women and children of all ages, sizes and levels of fitness need not be defenceless in the face of attack.

■ ■ ■ ■ What Exactly is Self Defence? ■ ■ ■ ■

In simple terms, self defence is a range of skills, both physical and non-physical, which are designed to ensure the safety and the physical wellbeing of a person who is the subject of an assault or a potential assault, or who otherwise feels in danger of any potentially threatening situation. At the core of my view of self defence is the concept of the 'ordinary, decent citizen', about whom I have made certain assumptions:

1. The ordinary decent citizen doesn't like violence and doesn't want to learn how to be good at it.
2. The majority of ordinary decent citizens don't have and don't want a martial arts background and are not necessarily going to be strong, fit or athletic.
3. Ordinary, decent citizens approach the learning of self defence not out of a desire to inflict harm *on* others but in order to avoid 'victim status' being inflicted on them *by* others.

My challenge was to create a system of self defence with such people in mind. This system has been adopted and is taught throughout the country by The British Self Defence Governing Body of which I am Chief Instructor. The skills taught in this book will equip you to be able to do the following:

1. Spot and avoid potential danger.
2. Neutralize, or render ineffective, a personal attack by the use of both non-physical and physical skills.
3. Be capable of bringing the attacker under control.
4. Make yourself safe.

Without any doubt, *preventing an attack* is the best form of self defence. With the help of this book, you will learn the skills needed to recognize and avoid danger, thus preventing you from becoming the victim of an assault.

> *'I must admit that at first I didn't like the idea of learning self defence. But after reading about so many people being assaulted, I thought I would give it a go. I haven't looked back since.'*

■ ■ ■ Types of Assault and How to Respond ■ ■ ■

The purpose of this section is to illustrate that your response to an assault should be determined directly by the nature of the assault you are subjected to and, although attacks can take various forms, the most typical take place in the following circumstances:

Mugging.
Sexually Motivated Attacks.
Domestic Violence.
Being Caught in the Midst of a Disturbance.

Taking each category in turn, I will explain the essential distinctions between them, so as to provide a useful insight into an assailant's mind and intention. I will also add my advice about how you should react in each case.

MUGGING

A mugging or robbery usually occurs when the assailant wants something you possess. This type of attack generally occurs on the street, although it can also take place in the home or in some other location. Typically, the assailant will not want a 'fair fight' and he will generally select as his victim someone who appears to be easy prey and easily intimidated. (Later in this book, I have included some practical advice about how you can avoid this so-called victim status.)

It would normally follow, therefore, that by giving up your possessions you could well reduce the prospects of being injured, although submitting to a mugger cannot be a guarantee of removing this risk altogether. Also, it is not uncommon for muggers to deny this opportunity to their victims and therefore a sound knowledge of useful self defence may be your only real chance of survival.

Advice:

■ Although there are almost as many variations to muggings as there are muggers, you should always consider giving up your possessions to avoid being injured. Remember, your possessions can be replaced – your life cannot.
■ Do not carry valuables with you unnecessarily.
■ Cover up expensive-looking jewellery.
■ Do not take short-cuts home and avoid deserted unlit areas and subways.
■ Do not hitch-hike or accept lifts from strangers.
■ Always walk facing on-coming traffic to avoid a vehicle sneaking up from behind you.
■ Carry your bag close to your body and, remember, always consider giving it up if someone grabs it. Just in case, carry your keys, cheque book and your credit cards in your pocket and, if possible, divide your cash among your pockets.
■ Don't make it easy for pickpockets. Carry your wallet or purse in an inside pocket if at all possible.
■ Carry a personal attack alarm to scare off an assailant, particularly if you are regularly out late or have to walk through isolated areas.

SEXUALLY MOTIVATED ATTACKS

As with most types of assault, those that are sexually motivated are also widely variable in their nature as well as their intent. This type of assault can usefully be divided into two categories. The first category is where the assailant is known to their victim and it is here where verbal and other non-physical skills are essential. The second category is where the victim is picked out by the assailant and is not known to him at all.

You will see on page 99 that recent research has suggested that in cases of sexual assault involving an assailant who is unknown to their victim those women who fight back actually *double* their chances of not being raped or seriously sexually assaulted. Therefore, to submit to an attack of this nature *can* be considerably more hazardous than to resist and fight the assailant off. It has been suggested that the long jail term the convicted rapist will receive will encourage his desire of avoiding capture, no matter what he has to do to his victim in order to evade detection.

Advice:

- Fight back. It is with assaults of this nature that fighting back can actually double your chances of not being raped and enhance your prospects of survival.
- Do not invite men into your home or your car, unless you know them well.
- Do not hitch-hike or accept lifts from strangers.
- Do not take short-cuts home and avoid deserted unlit areas and subways.
- Carry a personal attack alarm to scare off an assailant, particularly if you are regularly out late or have to walk through isolated areas.

DOMESTIC VIOLENCE

In a sense, domestic violence is the easiest type to deal with, because the assailant will be known to his victim. However, in another sense it is a most complex and painful problem and, accordingly, much of the violence continues for a considerable period of time.

Advice:

- Avoid alcohol and drugs in times of anger and anxiety within the home, particularly when you consider there is a possibility that there may be a discharge of anger through the use of violence.
- Where the violence persists and you consider that your only real option is to withdraw from the relationship, professional help is indispensable. I have included a section on domestic violence which you will find later in this book.

BEING CAUGHT IN THE MIDST OF A DISTURBANCE

To a large extent, being caught up in violence of this kind is preventable. It is not surprising to note that the majority of people manage to get through their lives without becoming involved with violence, whereas others seem unable to avoid it.

Advice:

- Be vigilant and alert to the possibility of danger. Even everyday situations can be life-threatening, so don't become complacent. This book contains extensive advice which will assist you greatly in avoiding violence and potentially dangerous situations.
- Don't ignore anything that you consider *could* mean danger. Assume that it does and react accordingly.

■ ■ ■ When Should You Use Self Defence? ■ ■ ■

The answer to this question is both simple and obvious to any decent-minded person whose only interest in self defence is to be able to defend him- or herself effectively and has no wish to perpetrate harm on anyone else. The physical self defence techniques taught in this book are to be used *only* when absolutely necessary and where all other means have failed. In other words, these techniques must be used *only* when you are in real physical danger.

A question that I am often asked is 'Should I surrender if I am ever attacked?' Although it would be impossible for me to provide a stock answer that could accurately cover every case, my considered general advice differs between a robbery-type of attack and a sexually-related one. In a robbery, where the assailant wants your possessions, giving them up *could* avoid involving you with any further violence. Whereas in a sexually motivated attack, recent research suggests that women who fight back actually *double* their chances of not being raped or seriously sexually assaulted and do not significantly increase their levels of injury. Therefore, in contrast to the myth that the rapist always succeeds, the evidence indicates that approximately 70 per cent of the women who fight back actually avoid being raped.

It has also been proven that those victims who do actively resist their assailant suffer far fewer psychological scars than those who surrender. But remember, fighting back covers a whole lot more than just the physical aspects of self defence. It includes the entire range of skills taught in this book. The physical aspects of self defence should only be deployed as a final resort.

I am afraid that if you are ever unfortunate enough to be faced with such an awesome predicament, then you must decide for yourself, and quickly, how you are going to respond. However, it is undeniable that the more proficient and confident you become in self defence the better your chances will be, no matter what decision you take.

Don't be fooled if the assailant promises not to hurt you if you do as he says. You really have no basis whatsoever for trusting a person like this to honour their part of the 'deal'. For your own safety, this type of 'promise' must be seen as being only superficially attractive. However, ultimately, it must be your decision, and you must be aware that, despite such a deal, your safety is far from guaranteed.

Some of the techniques taught in this book can cause considerable pain and injury to your assailant. Furthermore, in any physical confrontation, one can never foresee the end result. You could suffer injury yourself or you could injure your assailant. Therefore it is vital that you should avoid a physical confrontation wherever possible. If you are able to avoid a physical confrontation, then your safety is *guaranteed.* However, this of course is not always possible and, provided you are satisfied that a physical response cannot be avoided, it must be better to defend yourself effectively rather than face certain injury yourself. In these circumstances, you should not be concerned for your assailant; he is certainly not concerned about you. Your only concern should be your own safety. Even if it does mean that you might have to explain your actions at a later stage.

■ ■ ■ ■ The Psychology of Self Defence ■ ■ ■ ■

Attempting to teach self defence solely in terms of physical techniques while ignoring the raw emotions felt when a situation turns nasty is bound to fail. Techniques are applied by people, and people are highly emotional beings. A whole gamut of emotions are aroused when you realize that *you've* been chosen by someone to be *their* special victim! The feelings will range from panic to shock, to fear, to anger and to the anguished question of 'why me?'

BODY LANGUAGE AND SELF DEFENCE

Why me, indeed. It is a question well worth addressing. When a street thug selects you out of the crowd to be his next victim there are probably reasons for his choice. Thugs do not generally select people who look like they might be able to put up a fight. So your body language needs to exude confidence – not fear. If you look timid and easily intimidated you are marking yourself out as a natural victim. Therefore, simply cultivating an upright posture and a confident assertive walk will prove invaluable.

Body language, the basis of understanding one another without the aid of speech, is pretty much the same the world over. When we are happy we smile and, conversely, we frown to express our anger or unhappiness. Nodding or shaking the head also has its own meanings, as does the raising of one's fist in anger. However, just like any other language, body language consists of the equivalent of words and tone which, depending upon the circumstances, can have several different meanings. It is only when these words or the equivalent body language is interpreted as a complete 'sentence' that the meaning starts to become clear.

Body language is important in both avoiding trouble and in the de-escalation process of violent situations. Research carried out by Professor Ray Birdwhistell at the University of Louisville has shown that more human communication takes place by the use of gestures, postures and position than by any other method including speech itself. The benefit of positive words, therefore, is largely diminished by inappropriate body language.

A glance at the following table will show you just how important posture and tone are in body language when compared to the words actually used.

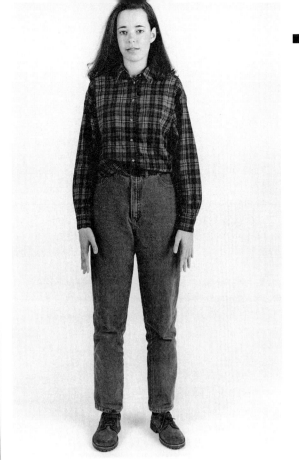

Fig. 1

Analysis of the perceived meaning of a message, comparing the words used to other non-verbal elements.

Words used	7 per cent
Non-verbal	55 per cent
Tone	38 per cent

Source: Findings by Albert Mehrabian and Professor Birdwhistell

---

To illustrate this point, take the example of a group of men attending a darts final in a pub. We are all familiar with the sort of 'male camaraderie' that is commonplace on such occasions! If the epithets which are regularly exchanged were to be taken literally, rather than in the spirit in which they were clearly intended, then it could quite possibly become unpleasant! The point is that it is the context and the implicit rules of behaviour which that context confers which define the meaning of the words used and the intentions of the user.

Body language can also be a *substitute* for verbal messages. For example, a woman can give a man a 'look that can kill', whereby she expresses her explicit message to him without actually opening her mouth at all.

A good example of a submissive, non-threatening attitude is shown in fig. 1. Here you can see the head is in the central or neutral position and the arms and legs are slightly apart. Notice how the lips are relaxed and are slightly

open. The palms too are open and the fingers are extended and widely spread to add impact to the gesture. You will see later how many of these non-threatening elements have been used in the self defence stances which, as well as preparing you for a possible physical confrontation, actually try to *de-escalate* the situation.

Compare this to the position portrayed in fig. 2. Here you can see a more aggressive posture being adopted. Observe the way the body is pointing directly at the other person and the way the hand-on-hips posture has been adopted. Notice how the face is pulled tight and the facial expression is consistent with the overall body posture.

Assertive body language is a vital part of our self-defence armoury. But what exactly does this mean? Just think about your everyday posture and about some of the signals that you give out – perhaps inadvertently. For example, how often do you present a smile, even when you are boiling over with anger? How often do you stoop or crouch, or shuffle your feet, or play with your hands or hair? It might be that you are trying to

Fig. 2

It is important to practise improving your overall body language. Think how you would look through someone else's eye. Do you look timid and afraid or do you give the impression of confidence?

You may find it useful to practise your body language skills with a friend. If so, look at each other critically and discuss the 'signals' that each of you are giving out. Try going out together for a couple of hours and then you will be able to observe and comment on each other more thoroughly.

By adopting an assertive and confident manner, you will be telling others that you are *not* victim fodder and that you know your own mind and will not be pushed around. *Above all, the message that you will be emitting is that you are not earmarked as a victim.*

> '*I have really enjoyed learning self defence and it has done wonders for my self confidence and morale. I now go out a lot more and am not frightened by the things that used to concern me.*'

BE ASSERTIVE

portray confidence or that you are just being playful. But be warned – all of these signals can easily be misread.

Ensure therefore that what you say or mean is not countermanded in any way by your facial expressions or by other messages given out by your body language.

Study the following table and see how many of the bad practices listed can be attributable to you, then study the good practices to improve your body language.

This book is about self defence and so it might be assumed that all the aggression has to come from the attacker. This is simply not so. Self defence is an act of self assertion. It is a refusal to accept 'victim status'. Some people are naturally more aggressive and assertive than others and so aggression and self assertion training are essential ingredients in self defence. It is no use being technically capable of applying a technique if you don't dare do it! Clearly, if one's physical ability was the only important ingredient in self defence, then we

BAD PRACTICES	GOOD PRACTICES
Hasty, nervous smile	Relaxed, confident smile and facial expression
Jumpy disposition	Relaxed and unruffled behaviour
Quiet, mumbling, uncertain voice	Secure, confident tone
Fidgety hands – always fiddling	Casual and relaxed hand movements
Stooped posture	Upright, relaxed and well-balanced posture
Nervous eye contact	Relaxed and steady direct eye contact

would never hear of frail old women seeing off attackers. Their determination not to fall victim to these thugs more than compensates for their lack of physical power and skill. In other words, they are exhibiting their assertive behaviour.

But what exactly is assertiveness? Assertiveness is a specific type of behaviour which assists us in communicating, clearly and confidently, our feelings, needs and desires. It is the opposite to passive behaviour, where our message is often lost either through our ambiguous or hesitant actions. With assertive behaviour, therefore, there can be no beating about the bush or vagueness. You know what you want and, more importantly, what you don't want. Communicate it – clearly.

Let us examine some typical assertive responses to unwelcome advances or threats. Remember, for these responses to stand a chance of working, they must be delivered with conviction and with the appropriate body language.

> 'I **don't** want you to do that to me!'
> 'You are **not** going to take my handbag!'
> 'I do **not** want to have sex with you!'
> 'Your behaviour is scaring me. Stop it, **now**!'
> 'I want you to leave my house, **now**!'

There is a well known assertiveness training technique called *Broken Record* whereby you repeat what it is that you want or don't want, over and over again, in a relaxed, assertive manner, until the other person either yields and accepts your position or walks away in sheer frustration. For this technique to be effective you should change some of your words, while ensuring that the message you are conveying remains the same. For example, 'You can't come into my house' can change to 'I'm not going to let you in' and to 'There's no point in standing there, I will not change my mind; you're not coming in' and so on until the message is finally accepted. The purpose, therefore, of using the *Broken Record* technique is to teach persistence, irrespective of the words you actually use, rather than to speak as though you were in fact the broken record itself.

Learning to say 'no' with conviction and meaning is also an important assertive skill. You will have read the previous section on body language and noted that your words can easily be countermanded by inappropriate body language, quite often inadvertently. However, there can be other reasons for your reluctance to say 'no': perhaps guilt, embarrassment or even shame. For example, you may feel that by saying 'no', the other person may stop liking you, or will feel angry or hurt, or will consider it rude. You may even consider, for whatever reason, that you have no right to refuse. All these fears can, and often do, lead to you saying 'yes' and regretting it afterwards.

Learn to be angry and reveal your anger to your assailant. As logical as this may sound, it is surprising how many people choose to display no anger at all, preferring 'anything for a quiet life'. *Anything?* This person has no right whatsoever to be doing this to you.

Most unassertive people accept other people's behaviour far too easily. However, you must accept that you *do* have an option. *Exert* your positive attitude and remember, you don't have to do anything that you don't want to. It is *your* life.

When it comes to an assault, a trained person isn't a superman who doesn't experience the same gut-churning fear as an untrained person. On the contrary – he does. Training involves self discipline and self control. It involves the ability to act appropriately despite being afraid. The confidence to control your fear and to channel it into a successful act of self defence is the reward of training and practice.

Lisa Sliwa and her husband Curtis run Guardian Angels, which has often been described as 'America's most celebrated public defenders'. She is trained in karate and yet it was her absolute determination, rather than her combat skills, that prevented her from being raped when she was attacked by three men in a building in New York that the Guardian Angels were renovating for the benefit of the city's homeless. As she puts it, 'I realized I had no time to feel sorry for myself. I made the decision that this man was not going to rape me. I knew I had one shot at an escape and it had to be right. My attitude was, I'm going to live and nobody is going to rape me.' Fortunately, she succeeded and saw off her assailants, one of them nursing painful testicles and a bitten thigh!

This next account of a real-life assault illustrates that your assertiveness and sheer determination to avoid assault is just as important as the physical skills, both of which, with the help of this book, you will soon develop.

'*Sharon is a keen jogger. One day, when she was out running, she sensed that she was being followed. This is what she said: 'At first, I tried to ignore him but he continued to follow me. I was so incensed that he would not let me enjoy my run in peace, that I turned around and yelled at him to stop following me. Although he swore at me and made crude suggestive remarks, he did, in fact, stop following me. The look of utter surprise on his face when I confronted him will be with me for a long time to come.*'

By adopting an assertive attitude, you are making it known that you know your own mind and will stand up for yourself and that, most importantly, *you* are *not* a victim.

In many instances, it will be better for you to take the initiative and exert your assertiveness, rather than to wait for a confrontation to develop, which could well lead to you facing a much more difficult and potentially hazardous predicament. As Robert Browning, the nineteenth-century English poet, once said, '*When the fight begins within himself, the man is worth something.*'

Assailants don't particularly want trouble and it is for this reason that they will select as their innocent victim someone who looks timid and would appear to be least likely to fight back. In other words, someone who has 'victim' stamped all over them.

Remember the old saying: 'It's not the size of the dog in the fight that's important, but the size of the fight in the dog!'

OVERCOMING FEAR AND THE 'FROZEN RABBIT' SYNDROME

Very often when people with no experience of self-defence techniques are attacked, the shock of being victimized in this way often results in what I term the 'frozen rabbit syndrome', whereby the victim virtually freezes in very much the same way as a rabbit freezes when caught in the headlights of a car. The victim then succumbs to the attack and

only afterwards thinks what he might have done. Very often he may suffer intense feelings of self-recrimination and guilt because he may feel, however wrongly, that he has acted in a cowardly fashion by not fighting back.

The fact is, however, that someone not experienced in dealing with street situations – and, let's face it, the vast majority of us fall into this category – has every right to feel afraid, and generally the confidence to deal with attackers is the product of learning and experience and not the result of some supposedly innate personal quality called 'courage'. The techniques taught in this book will help you to develop the confidence needed to deal with attackers effectively.

Just a little presence of mind can enhance your prospects of not falling victim to an assailant. It is vital that you stay calm as this will give you time to think and, if necessary, utilize your self-defence skills. The ability to respond in this way does require some degree of both technical ability and confidence and this is exactly what this book aims to provide.

Attitude is an extremely important factor in self defence. The *only* attitude you should have when faced with danger is one of surviving and succeeding. Remember, there are no prizes for being second best.

An assailant works on the assumption that he will be greeted by a stunned lack of resistance from his victim, thereby ensuring that the crime is over and done with before the victim knows what has hit him. Any complication and delay caused by the victim's resistance will, at the very least, throw the assailant off his stride, giving the victim valuable moments in which to either escape or otherwise further deal with the situation.

In other words, by the victim offering resistance, whether verbal, physical or both, the element of surprise will work very much against the criminal, in the same way that it was intended to work against the victim in the first place. This rationalism is the same, irrespective of the type of incident you are facing: muggers, bag snatchers, flashers, burglars – they all require the same element of surprise to achieve their objectives. Denying them this ingredient is the first step to being able to avoid becoming their victim.

Don't freeze; instead use the same vital ingredient as the criminal. Surprise.

> '*When I was attacked, I was determined not to allow the thug to succeed. I decided to fight back and to make it count. It did. I was able to get my attacker onto the ground and then I escaped to safety. I am convinced that it was the surprise of my self defence that allowed me to take the initiative and to defeat him.*'
>
> '*I have learned how to defend myself and so didn't freeze when I was attacked. I kept calm and found that what I had learned actually worked well. I can understand other women freezing with fear if they have never learned self defence. After my experience, I would recommend that everyone learns how to defend themselves.*'

■ ■ ■ ■ Avoiding Confrontations ■ ■ ■ ■

Being able to avoid a confrontation is far better than having to resort to any physical self-defence technique once violence has erupted. Accordingly, I have included a substantial amount of advice and information about avoidance in this book.

Many confrontations and assaults occur because the victim has shown that she is either *available* (in the wrong place at the wrong time), *accessible* (too easily approachable), or *vulnerable* (defence-less, drunk, afraid, nervous or maybe just too trusting). By eliminating these factors, you will greatly reduce the likelihood of becoming a victim.

Trying to reason with a possible attacker must always be considered as a first option. Even swallowing your pride is something to be commended. However, you must always be aware of the fact that the attacker could strike at any moment and you must always be ready to respond.

Reasoning with an attacker is a continuous process. Imagine a situation where, without any notice, you are attacked. You succeed in being able to apply one of the techniques taught in this book, and you now have control over your assailant. This could be the ideal opportunity for you to escape and make yourself safe, but it could prove to be too dangerous. You will, in the majority of cases, be in a position to choose the amount of force that you apply to your technique, which should always be decided upon in accordance with the severity of the situation. As you will now be out of immediate danger and in control of your assailant, you will have the opportunity of reasoning with him, with the intention of talking him out of further aggression towards you. As a final resort, you will know that, should it be necessary, you can always increase the amount of force that you apply to your technique.

You must always remember that although the material contained in this book will, with practice, hold you in good stead, the outcome of any violent confrontation will always be uncertain, no matter how proficient you are. The more you practise these techniques, the greater will be your chances of applying them successfully in a 'real life' situation.

Practise these techniques regularly and remember, use them only when reasoning with your assailant either fails or is impractical.

■ ■ ■ ■ De-escalating a Situation ■ ■ ■ ■

It is clear that your own actions are vital in order to de-escalate and take control of a violent or potentially violent situation.

One can look at many examples to portray this point and I will illustrate some hypothetical but regrettably all too common occurrences.

Imagine that you are driving your car when another vehicle pulls up in front of you and the driver gets out of his car to remonstrate with you. In an aggressive manner, he accuses you of nearly causing an accident. It would be all too easy to return the aggression – but where will it get you? Instead, try speaking in a firm, calm voice and explain that you were unaware of having done anything wrong. You might want to offer an apology – even if you feel it to be totally unwarranted.

Let us now consider what you should do if you are confronted by an aggressor who accuses you of staring at him. Again, you must speak to him in a firm voice and keep calm. Explain that you have no reason to be staring at him, or, if it is more appropriate, tell him that you thought you recognized him. Ask him if he can think of any reason why you should be looking at him. This is an important question to ask, as it puts the onus on the aggressor to explain why he has made such an accusation. It is most unlikely to inflame the situation and could prove to be extremely valuable in the de-escalation process.

A friend of mine once witnessed a case similar to this when he stopped at a service area on the M6 motorway, near Birmingham. The manager had been observing a gang of loutish youths when one of them, in an aggressive manner, uttered those immortal words: 'Are you looking at me?' The manager responded by asking, 'Can you think of any reason why I should be looking at you?' Somewhat lost for an answer, the youth quietly left the scene.

The point that this story illustrates is that the manager was able to control the situation by reversing the roles and, instead of justifying himself to the aggressor, he put the aggressor on the defensive by responding to his questions, not with answers but with other questions. This is a good example of how a mature person with a reasonable level of social skills can handle a situation verbally, which otherwise could have turned nasty.

The following is a list of do's and don'ts that will help you in the de-escalation process of any situation.

Do's

- Speak in a firm, calm voice. This will encourage the aggressor to do likewise.
- Listen attentively and interact regularly with him.
- Acknowledge the aggressor's point as soon as possible. Reflecting his feelings back to him will act to reassure him that you are listening and taking him seriously.
- Suggest that you move to another location if there is someone or something that is causing or increasing your aggressor's hostility.
- If possible, sit down with the aggressor, as this often leads to a lowering of tension.
- If the situation deteriorates, define the acceptable behavioural limits. For example, say something like, 'I'll continue this discussion with you but first you must stop shouting and swearing.'

Don'ts

- Don't shout or speak in a raised voice, as this will only encourage your aggressor to do likewise.
- Don't walk away or turn your back while the aggressor is talking to you.
- Don't invade the aggressor's personal space.
- Don't ignore or show inattention or indifference to the aggressor.
- Don't be condescending towards the aggressor and don't patronize him.
- Don't unnecessarily argue with the aggressor or utter threats of any kind. However, you can still maintain your position and put your points across to him.
- Don't give him orders, such as 'shut up' or 'sit down'.
- Don't use offensive language or make personal, hurtful or disrespectful remarks.
- Don't gesticulate: pointing, finger wagging or waving your arms around will only inflame the situation further.

■ ■ ■ ■ ■ Distraction Techniques ■ ■ ■ ■ ■

It is often useful to be able to distract your assailant and, if used correctly, the following techniques can give you valuable added seconds in which to make your escape. These tips can also distract your assailant sufficiently so as to leave him exposed to a counter-attack by you. Your assailant's response to your diversion techniques could vary greatly and the plausibility of your actions will largely influence his.

You can distract your assailant in a number of ways. For example, throwing some money on the ground might result in your assailant bending down to pick it up. This could give you vital seconds in which to make your escape or, if this is impractical, it could leave his face vulnerable to being kicked by you.

Alternatively, you could point to something that is out of your assailant's immediate line of vision. Consider pointing to an imaginary person behind your assailant and claiming it to be a policeman. If your assailant looks round, it could again give you valuable time in which to escape. By turning his head, he could be off-balance which would enable you to strike him on the side of his face, putting him further off-balance and giving you more time to escape. Remember, assailants do not want inconvenience or delay and they certainly don't want to have to deal with someone who is prepared to fight back.

Again, by pointing, you could pretend that some of your friends are approaching from behind your assailant. In addition to pointing, you could shout as if to summon their help, taking advantage of

your assailant's distraction as described above.

Another variation of the distraction technique is known as the feigning technique, which involves the carrying out of a ruse whereby, for example, you convince your assailant that you are about to give him something that he has demanded – this may be your purse or wallet or personal stereo – and when he attempts to take the item, you can use the opportunity to surprise him by slamming it into his face, groin or stomach, giving you valuable seconds in which to make your escape. This ruse can work particularly well because it appears that you are surrendering to your assailant's wishes and his own defence responses will be ill-prepared for the counter-attack.

Feigning can, of course, cause confusion as well as distraction. For example, pretending to kick the assailant in his groin will cause his body to bend forwards with his head down, in anticipation of the expected pain. Similarly, a feint to his eyes will cause him to blink and to withdraw his head. Both of these reactions leave him open to a counter-attack from you.

Feigning, of course, can take many different forms. It was reported in the national press on 28 May 1992 that when two raiders demanded cash from a postmaster in Broadstairs, Kent, the postmaster collapsed clutching his heart and shouted for them to call an ambulance. This caused the frightened raiders to flee empty handed. The postmaster was faking his collapse and, as the two men made their escape, he got to his feet, dusted himself down and calmly telephoned the police.

■ ■ ■ Physical Self-Defence Techniques ■ ■ ■

This section deals with the **physical** self-defence techniques needed to defend yourself against an aggressor.

Before beginning, it must be emphasized that a physical response is only to be used when everything else has either failed or when such **other actions would prove hazardous or could leave you exposed to danger.**

I have prepared each situation and corresponding defence with clear, step-by-step instructions enabling you easily to understand and learn what is being taught.

The self-defence techniques taught in this book can be used just as effectively against other types of attack as they can against the ones illustrated here. For example, the defence shown against a punch to the face can be used equally against any attack where the assailant reaches out towards you. Similarly, the techniques taught in the section Defences on the Ground can be used equally against a sex attacker or a mugger.

By now you should have read about the non-physical aspects of self defence and safety and you will have noted the emphasis that I have placed on trying to avoid a physical confrontation wherever possible. If, however, a physical confrontation proves to be unavoidable and you have no alternative other than to defend yourself physically,

then the easy-to-learn, minimum-force yet devastatingly effective techniques taught in this section may be employed.

Some of the techniques taught may appear to be unpleasant and you may feel that you could not bring yourself to carry them out. However, you must consider them in the light in which they are intended: when *you* are the victim of an assault. It is not a game. You may not have a second chance. Do not end up as another statistic. Defend yourself with all your ability and with an absolute determination to stop the assault and to survive.

The self-defence techniques taught in the following sections start with the assumption that you will have already adopted the appropriate stance. How to adopt a correct stance is dealt with after the following section.

■ ■ ■ How to Practise These Techniques ■ ■ ■

To enable you to practise the techniques in this book you will need a partner. However, before you begin to practise, it will be possible to get a reasonable understanding of what you are going to learn by reading through this book alone. This will also enable you to familiarize yourself with the techniques before you start to practise them with your partner.

Initially, until you are able to master the techniques with ease, your partner should assist you by not offering any resistance at all, and then gradually he should start to introduce some resistance against you until the technique works effectively in as near to a 'real-life' situation as possible. For example, once you have practised a particular technique, repeat the movement twelve times, with your partner increasing the level of resistance each time. Once you have managed to perform the technique effectively, try practising it on the move. Ask your partner to make the attack while he is moving and then, once you have completed the course, practise the techniques with your partner attacking in an unplanned manner. If possible, you should practise with partners of different sizes, abilities and strength. It is at this point that you

will be able to assess the effectiveness of your defence techniques.

You will find that you will prefer some techniques to others and that you will be able to perform some with greater efficiency. This is quite normal and with practice you should find that you have a good repertoire of effective self-defence techniques available to you to cover an extremely wide range of situations.

It is important to note that the techniques taught in this book are designed to defeat an often violent attacker and, therefore, when practising, great care must be taken not to inflict injury on your partner. Do not, for example, throw your partner forcibly to the ground or 'snap' on an armlock as you would in a serious real-life situation. Remember, you and your partner are helping each other to master these techniques.

Whoever is assuming the role of the attacker must make the attacks described as realistic as possible. It will be of little use, for example, when practising a defence, say, to a punch to the face, for your partner to stand with his arm outstretched, three feet from you and aimed wide above your shoulder. It is vital, therefore, that your partner distances himself so that when his arm is fully outstretched towards your face, his punch lands about six inches short of the target. This is to ensure that the punch is realistic, but does not injure you should your defence technique not immediately succeed.

Although your partner will know what your defence technique is going to be, your attacker will not. Therefore, at least initially, do not allow your partner to anticipate or avoid your defence. It is important that when applying any of these techniques in a real-life situation, you do not 'telegraph' your defence to your attacker, or indicate in any way what you are about to do.

The techniques in this book have been demonstrated on one side only. They do, of course, work equally well on the opposite side. When practising, it is important to do so on both sides.

The following sections of the book have been written carefully with a logical, progressive approach and it is important that you study them in the order that they have been presented. Please do not jump sections, as in many cases you will need to have read and fully understood the previous lessons before progressing further.

Finally, you should *never* assume that your first defensive response to an attack will be sufficient to deal with the situation adequately. You *must* always remain constantly alert, which will enable you to continue your defence techniques, should this prove to be necessary.

Practise the techniques regularly, as it is the constant repetition that will make you proficient in self defence.

■ ■ ■ ■ Adopting a Correct Stance ■ ■ ■ ■

Stance, in self-defence terms, is the position and posture that you adopt when you are facing an aggressor. As well as warning your aggressor that he is likely to be up against a knowledgeable opponent, a good stance will also assist you in maintaining good balance and will minimize the size and vulnerability of your body targets, while at the same time preparing your 'natural' body weapons for immediate use.

Together with the next three sections covering distance, evasion and blocking, you will learn the skills needed to protect you from your assailant's attack.

There are two types of stance you can adopt; one is to be used where you consider that there is a *possibility* of violence being used against you and the other is to be adopted where there is a threat of *imminent* violence. They are known as the **passive stance** and the **active stance** respectively.

The Passive Stance

The purpose of this stance is to reduce the size and vulnerability of your own body targets; to protect your body from attack by providing cover with your hands while ensuring that the stance is not hostile and will therefore not lead to an escalation of the situation. This stance will also help to prepare you should the prospect of violence become a reality.

To carry out this stance, position yourself to one side and at a slight angle to your assailant, with your feet shoulder-width apart, with one foot leading the other. Cross your hands in front of you and, keeping your hands open, cover your groin. Turn your head to look directly at your assailant, but do not neglect to observe your surroundings (fig. 3).

The Active Stance

This stance is to be adopted where there is an *imminent* threat of violence. Its purpose is to facilitate the immediate use of your 'natural' body weapons and to provide the best possible distribution of your balance. It also warns your assailant that he is dealing with someone with a knowledge of self defence, which in itself can be an effective deterrent. Like the passive stance, a clenched fist is not used, so as to avoid any unnecessary escalation of the situation.

To carry out this stance, adopt the same position

Fig. 3

Fig. 4

as for the passive stance but with your hips and shoulders squared so that the top part of your body faces on to your assailant. Raise your hands to chest height, with one in front of the other. Your palms should be open and your fingers together. If your right foot is leading your left, then ensure that your right hand also leads, and vice versa (fig. 4).

Some Additional Points About Stance

- Maintain a distance so that you are out of your

assailant's reach. This will mean moving about as your assailant moves. Distance will be covered in greater detail in the next section.
- Don't stand rooted to the spot. Your movements should follow his and should be carried out as quickly as possible, maintaining a stance as close as possible to your original stance.
- Keep your knees slightly bent and relaxed.
- Your movements should be steady and smooth – not jerky.
- Maintain good balance when adopting a stance and when moving around.

■ ■ ■ ■ Maintaining a Correct Distance ■ ■ ■ ■

Your stance *and* the distance that you maintain from your aggressor are vital if you are to avoid any attempt he might make at attacking you. By maintaining a correct stance and a distance that is out of your assailant's reach, you will be able to avoid his attack without too much difficulty,

thereby rendering it ineffective.

The correct distance that you should maintain between your assailant and yourself is approximately two arms' lengths apart. This will also give you sufficient additional time in which to react to the attack.

■ ■ ■ Evading Your Assailant's Attack ■ ■ ■

Evading an attack involves you moving in any direction in order to avoid it. Together with the correct stance, maintaining the right distance from your assailant and good evasion techniques, you will have an excellent chance of causing your assailant to miss you altogether. In simple terms, you are ensuring that you are an extremely difficult target to hit. Evading techniques are no more than removing your body from the line of your assailant's attack, thereby avoiding the attack altogether.

Imagine yourself standing at the centre of a giant clock face that has been painted on the ground. Your assailant is standing at the 12 position and it is from there that he will launch his attack. As the attack travels along the centre line towards you, you have the option of moving to either the 3 (to the right), the 6 (backwards) or the 9 position (the left). The choice is yours and will be determined largely by other factors, such as objects in the way, a busy road and so on. Of course, you are not limited to moving to the 3, 6, or 9 positions on the clock face; you can move to any other position depending upon the circum-

stances, provided that you do not move in towards the assailant.

However, as with most things, you will need to practise these skills thoroughly if you are to stand a chance of them succeeding in the event of a real-life situation. With your partner, one of you should assume the role of the assailant and attack with punches, kicks and grabs to various parts of the body, while the other tries to evade *but, for this exercise, I want you to use stance, distance and evasion techniques only as a means of avoiding the attacks.* **Ensure that you aim your blows at the target but that they land about six inches short of it, so that your partner does not get hurt, should the evasion techniques fail.** You will still be able to assess whether, in a real-life situation, you would have avoided being hit.

In the next section, I will examine the principles and skills needed to block your assailant's attacks which, together with the stance, distance and evasion techniques previously examined, will equip you with the ability to avoid his attack or at the very least, deflect it sufficiently to minimize its effects.

■ Blocking and Deflecting Your Assailant's Attack ■

By now, you will have learned the skills needed to *evade* an assailant's attack. Before commencing this section, let me add that, where possible, *evasion* must always be your priority and that blocking or deflecting the attack *reinforces* that position. Simply, if you have moved out of the way by the time the attack has reached you, you will not be caught by it. To strengthen your position, your arms also move to block or deflect the incoming attack. This is much the same as the actions you would take to protect yourself if a ball was kicked at your face.

The previous sections looked at stance, distance and evasion skills and this section explains the final stage in avoiding your assailant's attack. This

final stage is the block or deflection technique. Clearly, if your assailant's attack is to stand a chance of succeeding, you must be close enough for him to reach you and the path between you must be unobstructed.

A block or deflection is a means of intercepting and redirecting the assailant's attack, thereby knocking it off its course and preventing it from making good contact with you. You will also find that, by applying these skills correctly, your assailant will also be vulnerable to a counter-attack from you.

There are a number of blocks and deflections that can be used to prevent an attack from reaching its target, but unfortunately many of them can take a considerable amount of time before the user is able to defend himself adequately with them. The British Self Defence Governing Body, therefore, only uses two of these defences in its syllabus, which can be used effectively against a wide range of different types of attack, without having to dedicate years to their practice. They are known as the straight block and the cross block and are usually executed in conjunction with an evasion technique.

Where possible, you should elect to use the straight block in preference to the cross block, as by doing so you will also be removing your body from the line of fire by your side-stepping movement. The cross block is usually used where there is insufficient time to evade the attack in this way and with it you merely step *back* out of your assailant's range. An exception to this rule is where the attack is descending to the head, as in the case of a baton attack where the cross block should be used.

Irrespective of the type of block used, you should try to catch the incoming attack towards the end of the assailant's attacking limb. For example, a punch should be blocked near to the wrist and, similarly, a kick blocked near to the ankle. This can enable even a powerful attack to be halted without much effort.

To demonstrate this principle, ask your partner to stand with his arm outstretched, as though he has just thrown a punch at you. Ask him to resist, as hard as possible, any attempt you might make to move his arm. Now, place the palm of your hand on the side of his upper arm and try to move his arm from side to side. Difficult, isn't it? Now do the same thing, but this time move your hand to his wrist and see how much easier it becomes. Exactly the same will happen when blocking and deflecting your assailant's attack.

The Straight Block

The straight block is carried out by bending the elbow and deflecting the attack with an open palm, hitting the incoming attack *from the side* and knocking it off its course. This block usually uses the *leading* hand as it is the closest to the assailant, thereby having less distance to travel and ensuring the quickest dispatch.

Depending on the distance between you and the assailant when the attack is launched, the straight block can be carried out either with your arm bent at about 90 degrees or alternatively it can be executed with an almost straight arm. The 90 degrees block is used against attacks launched from a short distance, whereas the block with the straighter arm is used to deflect attacks launched from further away.

Practise the straight block by following these simple steps:

1. The assailant attacks you with a straight punch to your face, using his right fist.
2. You will have already adopted the active stance and will be leading with one foot and arm. Let us first practise this block assuming that you are leading with your right foot and arm (fig. 5).
   a. Pivoting on the ball of your right foot, step back and around with your left foot and place it on the ground, so that you are standing at about 45 degrees from your assailant.
   b. Deflect the blow with your right palm, slapping your assailant's attacking wrist and causing the strike to move off target. If your stepping action was carried out correctly, you will have evaded the punch anyway and the block is only a guard (fig. 6).
3. This time, we will practise this block from the left active stance (fig. 7).
   a. Pivoting on the ball of your left foot, step back and around with your right foot and place it on the ground, so that you are standing at about 45 degrees from your assailant (fig. 8).
   b. Deflect the blow with your left palm, slapping your assailant's attacking wrist and causing the strike to move off target. If your stepping action was carried out correctly, you will have evaded the punch anyway and the block is only a guard (fig. 9).

When using the straight block, you should tighten your muscles in your hand on impact so that it adds additional power to the deflection. Your palm should be open and your hand should be ready to grasp your assailant's clothing or body in preparation for your counter-attack.

Fig. 5

Fig. 6

Figs. 7, 8, 9

The Cross Block

The cross block is carried out by stepping back out of your assailant's reach and forming a cross with your arms. If the attack is aimed at your face, *raise* your arms to form the cross, thereby protecting your face from attack, and if it is aimed at your stomach or groin, the cross is formed by *lowering* the arms to protect that part of your body. If there is insufficient space to actually step back, then lean or move your body backwards while carrying out this block, ensuring that you maintain a good balance as you move. Keep your elbows close to your sides and, in the case of a cross block defending an attack to your face, your palms should be facing your opponent's body (fig. 10), whereas with a cross block defending an attack to your lower body, your palms should face your own body (fig. 11). In both cases, your hands should be open with your fingers together. Ensure that your block is not held too close to your body as this could allow the attack to penetrate through your arms and reach you. You will see in fig. 12 that the block is formed too close to the defender's body, thus allowing the attack to penetrate and strike its target, whereas in fig. 13 the block is executed correctly and the attack is deflected safely off its course.

Practise the cross block by following these simple steps:

1. The assailant attacks you with a straight punch to your face, using his right fist.
2. You will have already adopted the active stance and will be leading with one foot and arm. Let us assume that you are leading with your right foot and arm (fig. 14).
3. Step back with your right foot and, at the same time, raise both arms and cross them diagonally in front of your face, trapping your assailant's wrist in between your crossed wrists. Continue to raise your crossed arms and your assailant's arm will also rise, moving it above its intended target (fig. 13).

Fig. 10

Fig. 11

Cross Block showing distance of your hands from your body

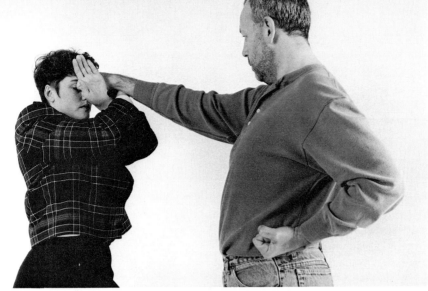

Fig. 12. INCORRECT

Fig. 13. CORRECT

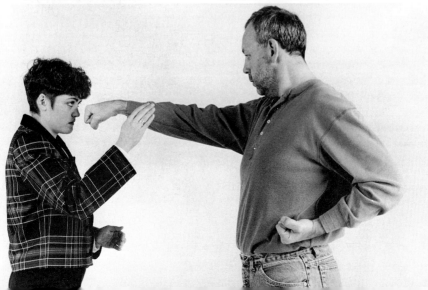

Fig. 14

The cross block can also be executed in a downwards movement to protect the lower parts of your body. Let us now practise it against a kick to the groin. Let us assume that you have adopted the right active stance.

1. Your assailant has aimed a kick at your groin with his right foot (fig. 15).
2. Step backwards with your right leg so that you are out of your assailant's reach and, at the same time, block the kick by crossing your forearms diagonally to trap his ankle (fig. 16).

It is important to remember that stance, distance and evasion will keep you out of your assailant's range and that a block is intended as a back-up to that principle. It is far better to move out of the way of your assailant's attack and then deflect it off course than to stand still and block it.

Now that you have read about the principles of stance, distance, evasion and blocking, it is important that you should practise these skills with your partner. As before, one of you should assume the role of the assailant and attack with punches, kicks and grabs to various parts of the body, while the other tries to evade and block the various attacks. *Ensure that you aim your blows at the target but that they land about six inches short of it, so that you do not get hurt should your evasion techniques fail.* You will still be able to assess whether, in a real-life situation, you would have avoided being hit.

As soon as you have evaded and deflected your assailant's attack, you should *immediately* initiate your counter-attack. Do not allow him time to recover his posture and balance or to overcome his shock. Take advantage of his weakness. The following sections deal with defences to a wide variety of attacks. Please ensure that you have understood and practised the previous sections thoroughly, before progressing further.

Before applying any physical self-defence technique, you must first stun your assailant by doing two things:

1. First, **shout out the words 'GO AWAY' as loud as you can.** This is designed not only to startle your assailant, but will also act to

Fig. 15

Fig. 16

intensify your own actions. It could also attract the attention of others, who could raise the alarm or come to your assistance. You must not be embarrassed about shouting this command. It could save your life. *Shouting is far better than just screaming as it delivers a clear message of your disapproval and condemnation.*

2. The second thing you must do *at the same time as shouting* is to cause your assailant to suffer **sudden sharp pain.** Allow me to explain the rationale for doing this. **Sudden sharp pain will momentarily halt most actions.** For this to work, the pain has to be sharp, for a dull pain can easily be ignored.

    To illustrate this point, consider the following. You are hammering a nail into a wall, when the inevitable happens – the hammer comes down on your fingernail. Or, you stub your bare toe on a door. Or maybe you slam your fingers in the door. The result of all of these mishaps is that you will suffer a sudden sharp pain and your actions will be momentarily halted. You will also suffer a temporary loss of control of your body movements and co-ordination.

    In a self-defence situation, this will enable you to apply the techniques more easily, because your assailant will have been distracted momentarily from his attack as a result of the sudden sharp pain that you have inflicted on him. He will lose control, temporarily, of his body movements and co-ordination. He may also withdraw, possibly permanently, from the attack, in much the same way as you would withdraw your injured limb in the above examples. For this to succeed, the pain must be sudden and sharp. You can cause it by any of the following actions:

- ■ Stamping hard on your assailant's foot.
- ■ Kicking him hard on his shins.
- ■ Kneeing or kicking him hard in his groin.
- ■ Biting him hard.
- ■ Jabbing him hard in his eyes.

    Or any number of other actions, depending upon the circumstances.

The pain that you inflict on your assailant also acts to reinforce the command that you shout at him. This is known as 'pain compliance'. It is important that you apply your self-defence technique immediately after you have caused this pain to your assailant. Do not give him time to recover. Another purpose of your shout and of causing this pain to the assailant is to overwhelm him *right from the start* with your sudden and unexpected counter-attack and to *discourage* him from continuing with the assault. It is also intended to make *him* worry about avoiding further injury himself and suffering embarrassment.

By responding immediately and powerfully to any assault, *you* will gain the advantage of surprise over your assailant, which will probably lead to *him* being momentarily paralysed and resulting in his change of priority from attack to escape. Remember, assailants usually don't want trouble and if they think that you will give it to them they will go and find another victim elsewhere who won't. After all, there are plenty of them about.

There is little doubt that even the most street-hardened among us will be taken aback by the unexpected nature of an assault. It is important, therefore, to help calm your nerves, that you should breathe slowly and deeply.

Never underestimate an assailant. You should always proceed on the basis that he is dangerous.

■ ■ ■ Body Targets – Where to Attack ■ ■ ■

It is important to know which parts of *your* body are vulnerable to an attack by an assailant. You also need to know which parts of *his* body will make the easiest and most effective targets for you to aim at. The following information is a useful guide to the various areas of the body that are exposed to such attack (fig. 17).

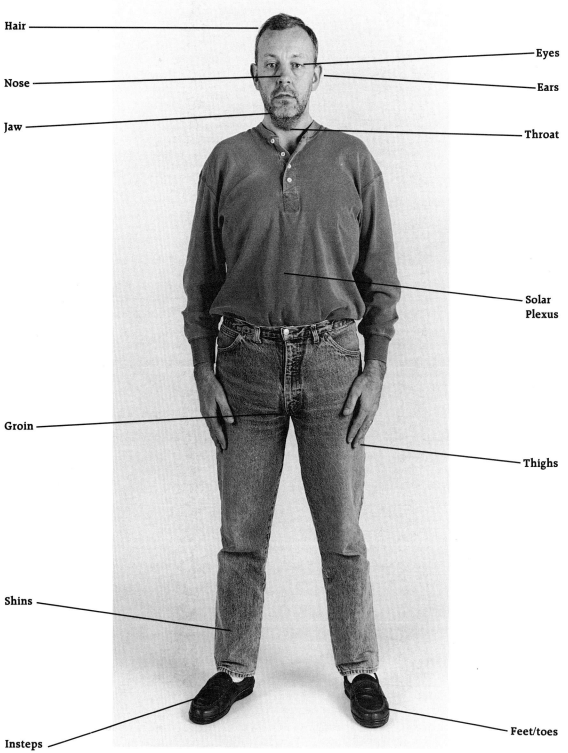

Hair

Nose

Jaw

Groin

Shins

Insteps

Eyes

Ears

Throat

Solar
Plexus

Thighs

Feet/toes

Fig. 17

1. **Hair** This can be pulled aggressively. Anywhere on the head will hurt, although the hair just above the sideburns and the hair just above the top of the neck are the most painful.

2. **Eyes** Eyes can be poked, gouged or pressed, even when closed. The natural reaction of the eyes is to close whenever something fast-moving approaches, and the head usually follows by withdrawing backwards. This reaction can prove to be invaluable, as a short distraction can allow you precious seconds to either escape or counter-attack. If your assailant closes his eyes, press them hard with your thumbs, increasing the pressure until his actions cease. Even feigning an attack to the eyes can provide an effective distraction, giving you valuable seconds in which to escape or mount a counter-attack.

3. **Nose** Striking at the nose or smashing it upwards can be very effective. To smash it upwards, strike your assailant under his nose with the heel of your hand forcing his head upwards and backwards.

4. **Ears** Ears can be pulled sharply or slapped aggressively. By cupping your hands and slapping both of his ears at the same time, you will cause considerable pain and disorientation.

5. **Jaw** Striking the side of the jaw can lead to loss of balance and/or unconsciousness. However, the mouth itself is not a good target, because of the damage the assailant's teeth can cause you. The teeth can also cause infectious wounds to the defender (fig. 18).

6. **Throat** A blow to the throat can cause difficulty with breathing. Attempting to strangle the assailant by squeezing his windpipe is not usually recommended as this usually causes the assailant to increase the level of his violence in an attempt to struggle free and is therefore more difficult to maintain. Pushing against the Adam's Apple is also useful as it could cause the assailant to withdraw his body from the assault. Applying a 'V' strangle with the crook of your elbow or a bar strangle with your forearm are also very effective (fig. 19).

Figs 18, 19, 20

7. **Solar plexus** Striking here can cause difficulty with breathing and can wind the assailant. Blows with the fist or heel of the hand are particularly effective, as are reverse-elbow strikes where the point of the elbow is used to strike the assailant (fig. 20).

8. **Groin** A blow to the groin can stun and incapacitate an assailant. The testicles themselves are particularly vulnerable and just a small blow can cause severe pain, which can spread rapidly to the muscles in the stomach. It is often difficult to grab the testicles because of the trousers, but if this is possible, then grabbing, squeezing and twisting can bring excruciating pain. Even feigning an attack to the groin can provide an effective distraction, giving you valuable seconds in which to escape or mount a counter-attack.

9. **Thighs** Grabbing, squeezing and twisting the pad of flesh on the inside of the thigh can cause sharp pain.

10. **Shins** Kicking the shins can cause severe pain, as can scraping them with a kicking, scraping action with your foot.

11. **Insteps** The insteps are vulnerable to being kicked, stamped on or scraped as described above.

12. **Feet/toes** Stamping on the feet or toes can momentarily disable your assailant and can also cause him to either raise or withdraw his injured foot, thus causing his balance to be impaired.

■ ■ ■ ■ Your Own Body Weapons ■ ■ ■ ■

Your own body has its own in-built weapons which can be used effectively against an assailant. This section looks at these 'natural' weapons and how they can be used to defend yourself. Practise these techniques regularly, so that the movements become easy to perform should the need arise. Remember, if you ever need to use these techniques, you should strike your assailant as hard as you possibly can. You may only have one chance. *Remember, you are being attacked!*

Fist

It is important to clench your fist correctly so that you do not injure your hand, wrist or fingers when striking your assailant. A correctly clenched fist starts with the tops of the fingers being bent inwards tightly, leaving your thumb up, and then bending your fingers once more to form a tight fist. Finally, fold your thumb down and across to lock and squeeze your fingers, ensuring that your thumb is not across the section of the fingers nearest to the knuckle.

With your fist, you can punch or strike your assailant in a number of ways (figs. 21, 22, 23).

Heel of Hand

Bend your fingers inwards and holding your palm upright, bend your wrist as far back as possible. With a punching movement, jab your assailant with as much force as possible (fig. 24).

Hand Claw

Make a claw with your hand by stretching your fingers and drive the hand into your assailant's face, forcing your fingers into his eyes and the heel of your hand into his nose and mouth (fig. 25).

Fingers

Slightly bend your index and middle fingers and, keeping them rigid, jab your assailant in the eyes. This move is very effective, due to its ease of operation and to the severe pain and discomfort it causes to the assailant. It can, however, cause serious eye injury and therefore it should only be used in extreme circumstances (fig. 26). Your fingers can also be used to pinch and twist your assailant's sensitive areas, such as his lips, ears, the inside of his thigh or indeed any other part of his body.

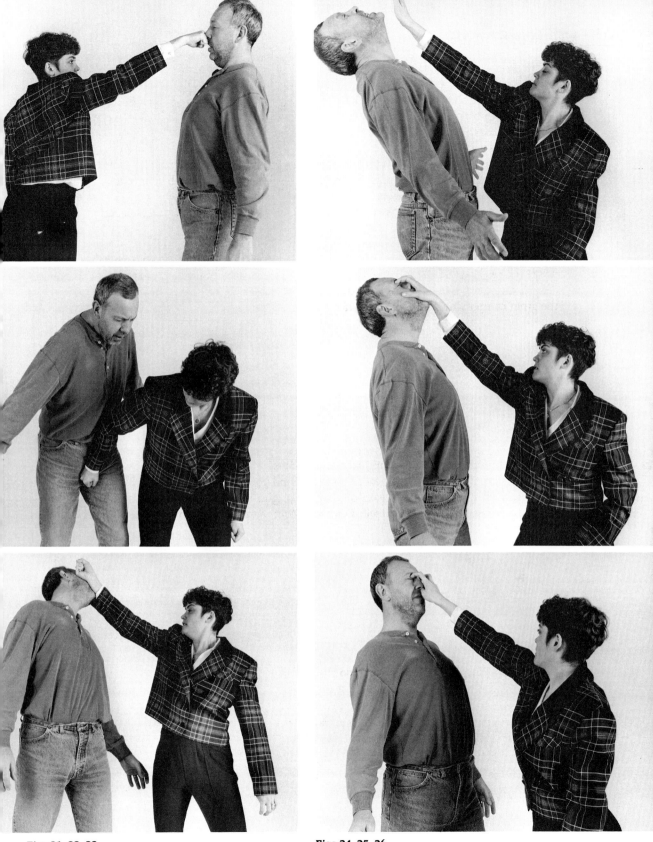

Figs 21, 22, 23

Figs 24, 25, 26

Elbow

Bend your arm as far as possible, so that it forms a point at the elbow. It is with this point that you strike your assailant. You can strike him with a forward or a backward blow. There are two simple forward strikes, one to hit your assailant on the side of his face and the other to hit him under his jaw. To strike him on the side of his face, move your arm in a semi-circle and strike him on the side of his jaw (fig. 27). To hit him under his jaw, your arm starts in a vertical position and then you tilt your arm so that your elbow strikes your assailant under his jaw (fig. 28). To use your elbow in a backward strike, extend your arm forwards and then strike your assailant by driving it backwards sharply into the target (see fig. 20 on p. 33). In all elbow strikes, you should follow your striking movement by following through with your shoulders and hips and you should always keep your fist clenched.

Knee

You can strike your assailant with the top of your knee, usually in his groin. Ideally, this strike is best performed when your assailant's body is very close to your own, such as when he has his arms around you. This will prevent his natural reaction of protecting his groin with his hands (fig. 29).

Feet

Your feet can be used in a number of different ways. To **kick** your assailant, curl your toes upwards to avoid them being injured and snap your foot at the target, hitting it hard. You should kick with the ball of your foot (fig. 30). As soon as you have delivered the kick, bring your foot back to its original position so as to regain your balance and to avoid your assailant grabbing hold of it. You can also strike your assailant with a rear kick by raising one leg and bending the knee, then snapping the foot back to hit the target. You can also use your feet to **stamp** on your assailant's foot. You should use your heel to carry out this move, which will be even more effective if you are wearing stiletto-type heels. Your heel is also used

Figs 27, 28, 29

Figs 30, 31, 32

to **scrape** your assailant's shin or instep and this can be done in conjunction with another kicking or stamping action.

Head

Drive either your forehead or the back of your head into your assailant's nose. Where possible grab hold of his head first, as this will enable you to hit your target more easily (fig. 31).

Teeth

Your teeth are useful for biting your assailant. Any part of his body can be bitten and you should choose the part that is closest to your mouth. Bite hard. Remember that it is the sudden sharp pain that will momentarily halt your assailant's actions (fig. 32).

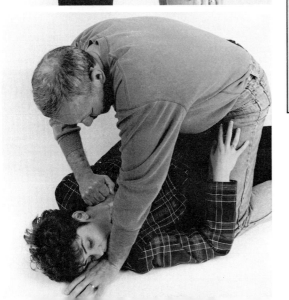

'*At first, I didn't think that I could bring myself to carry out these moves. After all they are not very pleasant, are they? But that was before I was attacked. I was furious and laid into my attacker with everything I had learned and with as much force as I could muster. It worked. My attacker fled, nursing the damage that I caused to his eyes with my fingers. I am so pleased that I learned self defence. I now know that if I am ever unfortunate enough again to be attacked, I can defend myself.*'

■ ■ Falling Correctly and Practising Safely ■ ■

Some of the self-defence techniques in this book result in your assailant either falling or being thrown to the ground. This section shows you how to break your fall correctly and therefore avoid injury. Remember that when you are practising these techniques with your partner you are helping each other, so great care must be taken to avoid injury. When *practising* a defence that involves a throw or takedown, do not apply it with force, but remember, in a *real-life* self-defence situation you should apply the technique with full force.

It would be ideal if you had some gymnastic-type mats on which you could practise or, if this is not possible, use a room that has thick carpeting. Ensure that you clear sufficient space so that you do not bang into anything and take care with low-hanging light fittings. Do not practise near sharp edges or glass doors or panels.

In this section, I will cover three basic breakfalls. One to the front, one to the rear and one to the side. Please note that these breakfalls are slightly different to those taught in martial arts like *judo*. This is because they are designed to be used on harder surfaces.

Front Breakfall (fig. 33)

Practise this from a kneeling position with the top part of your body upright. Turn your head to one side, so that you do not bang your nose on the ground. Lower and drive your upper body forwards, keeping your elbows bent and close to your body. Your palms should be facing downwards and the backs of your hands in front of your face, with your fingers straight and close together. Ensure that your arms and hands touch the ground *before* any other part of your upper body, and that they protect your face and prevent it from hitting the ground. Do not bend your wrists or reach for the ground with straight arms. Practise this a few times until you feel confident and then attempt it from a half-squatting position. Continue to practise this breakfall until you feel comfortable with it.

Rear Breakfall (fig. 34)

Starting from a squatting position, roll backwards, tucking your chin into your chest as you do so. This will prevent you hitting your head on the ground when you fall. After you have practised this a few times, repeat it and this time slap the ground with both hands and arms, ensuring that they touch the ground *before* any other part of your body. Your arms should start from a bent position with your hands in front of your chest. Your arms should be perfectly relaxed until they strike the ground. When you strike the ground, your palms should be facing downwards and your fingers straight and close together. Do not bend your wrists or reach for the ground with straight arms or your elbows. Practise this a few times until you feel confident and then attempt it from a half-squatting position. Continue to practise this breakfall until you are comfortable with it.

Side Breakfall (fig. 35)

Begin this exercise by lying on your back. Bend your knees and roll your body sideways from hip to hip. After you have done this a few times, slap the ground with your hand and arm, ensuring that

Fig. 33

they touch the ground *before* your body comes to a halt. The arm that you use to break your fall is the one *nearest* to the side where you are falling. In other words, if you are falling to your right, use your right hand to break the fall. Your arm should start from a bent position with your hand in front of your chest. Your arm should be perfectly relaxed until it strikes the ground. When you strike the ground, your palm should be facing downwards and your fingers straight and close together. Do not bend your wrist or reach for the ground with a straight arm or your elbow. Practise this a few times until you feel confident and then attempt it by rolling from hip to hip, slapping the ground each time. Continue to practise this breakfall until you are comfortable with it.

With all of these techniques, ensure that you do not bang into something or hit your head when you fall.

Also, please remove any watches, jewellery and any other hard or sharp items that could cause cuts or other injury. For similar reasons, your pockets should be empty.

If your partner submits or informs you that any technique that you are applying is causing pain or discomfort, you must stop the technique *immediately*.

For ease of study and to ensure that you achieve a greater level of understanding and application of the techniques, I have grouped them into the following categories:

1. **Defences Against Blows**
   Covering defence techniques against punches and kicks.

2. **Defences Against Being Grabbed or Held**
   Covering defences against being held or grabbed, bear-hugs, wrist holds and clothing grabs and including how to escape from being tied up.

3. **Defences Against Strangles and Headlocks**
   Covering defences to strangles, chokes and headlocks.

4. **Restraining Techniques**
   Covering techniques for restraining an aggressive assailant, including restraining an assailant who is attacking a third party.

5. **Defences Against Attacks Connected With a Motor Vehicle**
   Covering techniques to deal with attacks when you are either in or are about to enter the vehicle.

6. **Defences Against Weapon Attacks**
   Covering defences to deal with baton and knife attacks.

7. **Defences on the Ground**
   Covering groundwork defences and ground restraining techniques, and defences against rape and other sexually motivated attacks.

Fig. 34

Fig. 35

■ ■ ■ ■ ■ Defences Against Blows ■ ■ ■ ■ ■

Please remember that you should, where possible, already be in the *active stance* when facing these attacks.

DEFENCE AGAINST A PUNCH TO THE FACE

Attack

Your assailant has attacked you by throwing a punch at your face with his right fist.

Defence 1

1. Stepping backwards to move out of your assailant's range, raise both arms in an upwards diagonal movement and cross your forearms to trap his fist. Continue to raise your crossed arms and your assailant's arm will also rise (see fig. 13 on p. 29).
2. Separate your arms outwards and grab hold of his wrist with your left hand (fig. 36).
3. Step forward with your right leg and, lunging forward with your right arm, strike your assailant under his chin with the heel of your hand, forcing his head backwards (fig. 37).
4. With your right hand, grab his clothing near to the top of his left shoulder and step well forward with your left leg, placing your left foot firmly on the ground to the outside rear of his right leg. Step forward with your right leg and, moving it behind his legs, place it on the ground behind his legs. Force him over your right leg by pushing with your right arm and sweeping backwards with your right leg. Lean forward with your upper body as you throw him backwards (fig. 38).

Figs 36, 37, 38

Defence 2

1. Stepping backwards to move out of your assailant's range, raise both arms in an upwards diagonal movement and cross your forearms to trap his fist (see fig. 13 on p. 29).
2. Separate your arms outwards and encircle his right arm by moving your left arm in an anti-clockwise rotation, continuing this circular movement until your left hand is near your own right shoulder. Your assailant's right arm should now be trapped under your left armpit. His right elbow will be held in a painful lock by pulling upwards with your left arm (fig. 39).
3. With the heel of your right hand, strike your assailant under his chin (fig. 40).
4. With your right leg, reach behind and past your assailant's legs and throw him backwards by sweeping his legs with your right leg. Assist the throw by pushing his head backwards with your right hand (fig. 41).

Armlocks work on the principles of leverage and therefore only a modest amount of pressure is required to control and defeat an aggressor, even one considerably larger and heavier than you.

Figs 39, 40, 41

DEFENCE AGAINST A PUNCH TO THE STOMACH

Attack

Your assailant has attacked you by throwing a punch at your stomach with his right fist.

Defence

1. Step backwards so that you are out of your assailant's reach and block the punch by crossing your forearms diagonally and sweeping them downwards to trap his fist in between them (fig. 42).
2. Step forward with your left leg and place your left foot on the ground, to the outside of his right foot. Your knees should be slightly bent.
3. Separate your arms outwards and encircle his arm with your left arm in an upwards clockwise direction and place your left hand, little finger facing downwards, on the back of his upper arm, ensuring that his forearm is trapped in the crook of your left arm (fig. 43).
4. Move behind your assailant, placing your right hand on the front of his right shoulder, ensuring that his right elbow bends 90 degrees, and, with your right hand, force him backwards towards you so that there is no gap in between your bodies (fig. 44).
5. Apply pressure to his right elbow by moving your left arm upwards and continue to pull him backwards with your right hand (fig. 45).

Fig. 42

Figs 43, 44, 45

DEFENCE AGAINST A KICK

Attack

Your assailant has aimed a kick at your groin with his right foot.

Defence 1

1. Step backwards so that you are out of your assailant's reach and at the same time block the kick by crossing your forearms diagonally to trap his ankle (fig. 46).
2. Grab his ankle with your left hand and lift his leg as high as you can. At the same time, step forward with your right leg, bending your right knee, and throw your assailant backwards by striking him under his chin with the heel of your right hand while continuing to lift his left leg (fig. 47).
3. Ensure that this defence is applied quickly, so that your assailant does not have a chance to regain his balance by putting his right foot back on the ground.

Figs 46, 47

Defence 2

1. Step backwards so that you are out of your assailant's reach and at the same time block the kick by crossing your forearms diagonally to trap his ankle (fig. 46 on p. 43).
2. Step forwards with your right leg and place your right hand around your assailant's waist. Your right knee should be bent (fig. 48).
3. Push the heel of your left hand under your assailant's chin and push him backwards, while pulling him forwards at the waist with your right hand, and you will be able to push him off balance, toppling him backwards to the ground (fig. 49).
4. Ensure that this defence is applied quickly, so that your assailant does not have a chance to regain his balance by putting his right foot back on the ground.

Figs 48, 49

Defence 3

1. Side-step the kick by pivoting on your left foot and stepping back with your right leg so that you are standing at 45 degrees to your assailant (fig. 50).
2. At the same time, catch his right ankle with your right hand and place your left hand on his right shoulder to prevent him from punching you (fig. 51).
3. Strike your assailant under his chin with a palm strike, using your left hand, and lift his right leg as high as you can, throwing him backwards to the ground (fig. 52).
4. Ensure that this defence is applied quickly, so that your assailant does not have a chance to regain his balance by putting his right foot back on the ground.

Figs 50, 51, 52

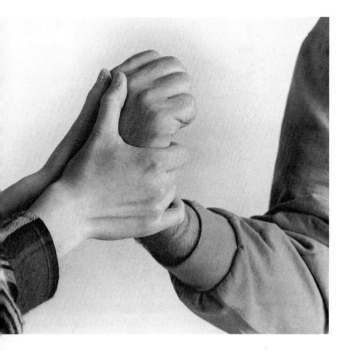

DEFENCE AGAINST A THREATENING FIST

Attack

Your assailant, who is facing you, has raised his fist in a threatening manner.

Defence

You have not been attacked. This is an ideal opportunity to use the non-physical responses taught in the book. You might even have the opportunity of escaping. The defence taught here is to be applied only in situations where you believe an attack is imminent and that you are in danger.

1. Grab your assailant's fist with both hands in such a way that your thumbs are on the back of his hand and your fingers are round the edge (fig. 53).
2. Pull his hand sharply towards your stomach, so that your own wrists are actually touching your stomach (fig. 54).
3. Bend his wrist inwards by pushing with your thumbs and you will have applied a painful wrist lock. You may find it helpful to take a step backwards when applying the lock, in which case you must ensure that your own wrists still remain in contact with your stomach. If you choose to take a step back, ensure that there is nothing behind you that could make you lose your balance or fall.

Figs 53, 54

DEFENCE AGAINST A FRONTAL ATTACK OR FRONTAL THREAT

Attack

This defence is particularly useful against any type of frontal attack or where you are being threatened from the front.

Defence

1. Cup your assailant's chin with your right hand and, at the same time, reach round the back of his head with your left hand and grab his hair, or alternatively the back of his head (fig. 55).
2. Step backwards with your left leg and simultaneously, with both hands, rotate his head in an anti-clockwise direction, forcing him to the ground (fig. 56).

Figs 55, 56

■ ■ Defences Against Being Grabbed or Held ■ ■

Please remember that you should, where possible, already be in the *active stance* when facing these attacks.

It is important to try to prevent your assailant from grabbing both of your hands at the same time, as this will reduce your ability to defend yourself.

DEFENCE AGAINST A FRONTAL HAIR GRAB

Attack

Your assailant, while facing you, grabs your hair with his right hand.

Defence 1

1. Place both of your hands on top of your assailant's hand, pressing it tightly onto your head. This not only prepares you for the defence but will also reduce the pain from the attack, as the pain is caused by your assailant's pulling action (fig. 57).

2. Sharply drop on to one knee while at the same time bend your upper body forwards and lower your head. Ensure that you maintain pressure on your assailant's hand, keeping it pressed tightly onto your head. The more sharply you drop on to your knee, the more effective this technique will be (fig. 58).

3. Your assailant should now be leaning forward towards you and his wrist will be bent backwards. Remove your hands from your assailant's hand and at the same time grab both of your assailant's legs from behind each knee, pulling them in towards your body while at the same time launching your body towards him, throwing him backwards to the ground (fig. 59).

Fig. 57

Fig. 58

Fig. 59

Defence 2

1. Place both of your hands on top of your assailant's hand, pressing it tightly onto your head (fig. 57).
2. Bend your upper body forwards and lower your head, while at the same time take several steps back. Ensure that you maintain pressure on your assailant's hand, keeping it pressed tightly onto your head. Your assailant's wrist will be bent backwards (fig. 60).
3. Keep moving backwards until your assailant is flat on the ground, face down (fig. 61).

Figs 60, 61

Defence 3

1. Grab his right wrist with your own right hand and keep his hand close to your head to ease the pain of the attack (fig. 62).
2. Place your left hand on the outside of his right elbow and, by pivoting on your left foot and stepping back with your right foot, turn your body to the right (fig. 63).
3. Push down hard with your left hand against the outside of his elbow and it should be easy to take your assailant to the ground with a very painful armlock. Ensure that the pressure on his elbow is applied *against* the normal joint movement (fig. 64).

Figs 62, 63, 64

DEFENCE AGAINST A REAR HAIR GRAB

Attack

Your assailant grabs your hair from behind with his left hand.

Defence

1. Place both of your hands on top of your assailant's hand pressing it tightly onto your head (fig. 65).
2. Step forward with your left foot and, pivoting on the balls of both feet, turn your body in a clockwise direction, so that you face your assailant. As you turn, lower your head and bend your upper body forward (fig. 66).
3. Keep your assailant's hand tightly pressed against your head and stand upright, applying a painful lock to his wrist (fig. 67).
4. Raise your left knee and drive it hard into his groin (fig. 68).

Fig. 65

Figs 66, 67, 68

Fig. 69

DEFENCE AGAINST BEING HELD BY YOUR WRIST (OR WRISTS)

Attack

Your assailant has grabbed your right wrist with his left hand.

Defence

1. This defence works by pulling your own wrist *sharply* towards yourself, in the direction of your assailant's thumb, which is the weakest part of his grip. This will cause his grip to loosen and so enable you to withdraw your hand. You should use a sudden sharp movement when pulling your hand free (fig. 69).
2. The same defence is used if you are being held by both wrists. In this situation, you will notice that your assailant's thumbs are facing each other. Before commencing the defence, try bringing your own wrists together sharply and smashing his thumbs together. When applying the defence, do remember to pull against your assailant's thumbs.

DEFENCE AGAINST REAR BEAR-HUG: YOUR ARMS FREE

Attack

Your assailant has grabbed you from behind by placing both of his arms round your stomach and is holding you tightly in a bear-hug. Both of your arms are free.

Defence 1

There is little point in trying to pull away from this powerful hold, as this is likely to achieve nothing other than wasting your own energy.

1. Bending the top part of your body sharply forward, reach between your own legs and, with both hands, grab hold of one of your assailant's legs, near to his ankle. With a sharp pulling movement, lift his leg as high as you can and at the same time straighten your own body thus throwing him backwards (fig. 70).

2. You will find it easier to bend your upper body forward if you first raise one leg forward in front of you, as though you were kicking an imaginary assailant. As you place your leg on the ground again, place it so it is behind your assailant's legs. This will make it easier for you to grab his ankle to throw him backwards (fig. 71).

Figs 70, 71

Defence 2

1. With your left arm, reach across your stomach and grab your assailant's right arm above his elbow. Ensure that his arm remains close to your body (fig. 72).

2. Step back with your right leg, so that it is on the outside of and behind his right leg, and bend your knees slightly. Ensure that your hips are in between his legs and are *not* blocking his right leg. At the same time, lean forwards and place your right hand as close to the ground as possible near to your own left foot. Ensure that your left arm has kept your assailant's right arm close to your body, so that there is no space between his chest and your back. This is essential for this defence to succeed (fig. 73).

3. Twist your body to your left and try to place your right hand on the ground about twelve inches in front of your own left foot and throw your assailant over your body and outstretched right leg, which you should straighten as the throw commences, and he should land on his back in front of you (fig. 74).

Figs 72, 73, 74

Defence 3

Turn the top part of your body towards your assailant and strike him on the side of his face with the point of your elbow (fig. 75).

Fig. 75

DEFENCE AGAINST A REAR BEAR-HUG: YOUR ARMS TRAPPED

Attack

Your assailant has grabbed you from behind by placing both of his arms round your stomach and is holding you tightly in a bear-hug. Both of your arms are trapped.

Defence

1. Move your left leg to the left, bending your knees deeply to lower your body and, at the same time, force both of your arms sideways and upwards so that your assailant's arms lift over your shoulders (fig. 76).
2. With a sharp movement, raise your arms vertically, to force your assailant's arms over your head (fig. 77).
3. Bend your right elbow and strike him in his solar plexus, by twisting your body to your right, stepping towards him as you do so (fig. 78).
4. Follow this with a hammer fist to his groin, using your right arm. Ensure that you strike him with the part of the fist that is furthest away from your thumb (fig. 79).

   You could find this defence a little tricky to master at first, but it is extremely effective, so perseverance will prove to be worthwhile.

Figs 76, 77

DEFENCE AGAINST A FRONT OR REAR BEAR-HUG: YOUR ARMS TRAPPED

Attack

Your assailant has grabbed you, either from the front or from behind, by placing both of his arms round your stomach and is holding you tightly in a bear-hug. He has lifted you off the ground. Both of your arms are trapped.

Defence

1. Move your arms and legs in much the same way as you would if you were running in a race (fig. 80).
2. By continuing with this running action, your assailant will have great difficulty in maintaining his grip on you, and you should be able to either escape from or severely weaken his grasp. As you are 'running', try to kick him.
3. As soon as his grip has weakened sufficiently, either strike him hard in his solar plexus with your elbow or, in the case of a front hold, strike him hard in his groin with your knee.

Fig. 80

Figs 78, 79

DEFENCE AGAINST AN UNWELCOME ARM ROUND YOUR SHOULDER

Attack

Your assailant has put his left arm round your shoulder.

Defence

1. Starting with your arms by your side, raise your right arm backwards and in an anti-clockwise rotation trap your assailant's left arm by placing the crook of your elbow against the outside of his elbow (fig. 81).
2. Continue with your anti-clockwise movement until your own right arm is against your stomach, and your assailant's arm is trapped by his elbow. You will now have applied a painful armlock to his left elbow (fig. 82).
3. Raise your left hand and place it on your assailant's left elbow. By stepping backwards with your left foot you will be able to add greater power to the armlock (fig. 83).

Figs 81, 82, 83

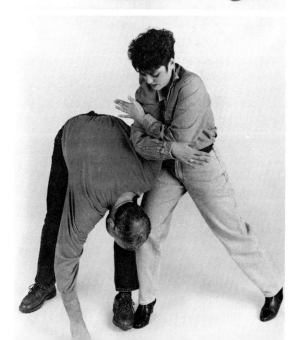

DEFENCE AGAINST A BAG OR PURSE SNATCH

Attack

Your assailant grabs hold of your bag or purse.

Defence

Most people when faced with this situation would attempt to enter into a 'tug-of-war' contest with the snatcher. Don't. The more you pull, the more he will, and if he is stronger, he will win. Try this defence instead!

1. Keeping a tight grip on your bag, push it hard into your assailant, aiming for a vulnerable area such as his stomach, groin or face. *This should be easy, because you are pushing in the same direction as his pulling action* (fig. 84).
2. At the same time, kick him hard on his shins and, if possible, follow this by kneeing him in the groin (figs. 85 & 86).
3. As soon as he appears stunned by your defence, grab your bag and drive it into his face (fig. 87).
4. You should now be able to make your escape.

Fig. 84

Figs 85, 86, 87

DEFENCE AGAINST A CLOTHING GRIP

Attack

Your assailant has grabbed hold of your clothing.

Defence 1 (assailant grabbing with his left hand)

1. Take hold of your assailant's left wrist with both hands (fig. 88).
2. Step back with your left foot and place it behind your right foot. At the same time, turn your body anti-clockwise. Keep your assailant's hand pressed tightly against your chest. Place your right elbow (which should now be bent) on top of your assailant's left arm near to the outside point of his elbow (fig. 89).
3. Press downwards with your right arm to apply an armlock. At the same time, position your left hand so that your thumb is on the back of his hand and your fingers are round the edge, and press his wrist in on itself. By continuing to apply pressure on his arm and wrist, you should be able to force him to the ground (fig. 90).
4. You may find it helpful to step across with your right leg and place it in front of your assailant's right leg (fig. 91).

Fig. 88

Figs 89, 90, 91

Defence 2 (assailant grabbing with his right hand)

1. Raise your right hand and place it on top of your assailant's hand, gripping over the edge of his palm, so that your thumb is on the back of his hand and your fingers are round the edge (fig. 92).

2. Peel your assailant's hand from your clothing by rotating his hand clockwise. Ensure that your thumb is still on the back of his hand and that your fingers continue to grip his palm (fig. 93).

3. Bring your left hand into the corresponding position on his hand and sharply push on the back of his hand with both of your thumbs and apply a painful wrist lock by bending his wrist inwards (fig. 94).

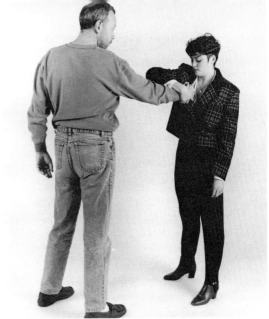

Figs 92, 93, 94

Defence 3 (assailant grabbing with both hands)

1. Raise your right arm in the air and step back and round with your left foot (fig. 95).
2. Bring your right arm over both of your assailant's arms, trapping them and pulling him forwards and off-balance (fig. 96).
3. Bend your right elbow and strike your assailant with a back elbow blow to the side of his face. As you strike your assailant, turn your head to face him, as this will help you to hit your target more accurately and will also add more power to the strike (fig. 97).

Figs 95, 96, 97

Defence 4 (assailant grabbing with both hands)

1. Raise one knee and drive it as hard as you can into your assailant's groin, or if he is bending forward and his groin is out of your knee's reach, kick him in his groin, ensuring that you snap your foot back as soon as the kick has been delivered, to prevent him from catching hold of your leg. The force of this blow should cause his upper body to bend forward (fig. 98).
2. Grab his head with both hands and force it downwards. Using the same leg as before, raise your knee and drive it hard into his face, while continuing to pull his head down with your hands (fig. 99).
3. You should now be able to make your escape.

Figs 98, 99

DEFENCE AGAINST AN ATTACK WHILE SEATED

Attack

You are seated and an assailant has grabbed both of your lapels and is attempting to drag you out of your chair.

Defence

1. Do not attempt to resist your assailant's pulling movement or break his hold from your clothing. Instead, as you are being pulled up, maintain your balance and rise at an angle to him (fig. 100).

2. Bend the elbow that is nearest to your assailant and strike him hard in his solar plexus. To ensure that this strike is delivered with sufficient force, first bring your arm forwards and clench your fist tightly (fig. 101).

3. If necessary, follow this blow by slamming him in his groin with a hammer fist, using the same arm that delivered the elbow strike. Ensure that you strike him with the part of the fist that is furthest away from your thumb (fig. 102).

4. Alternatively, or, if necessary, in addition, strike your assailant in his face with a back fist, still using the same hand as before (fig. 103).

Fig. 100

Figs 101, 102, 103

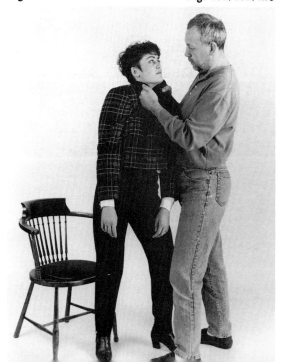

■ ■ ■ How to Escape From Being Tied Up ■ ■ ■

The first thing to remember is that you must, wherever possible, resist all attempts to tie you up or to gag you. It will be much more difficult to defend yourself if you do not have the free use of your limbs and, if you are gagged, you will not be able to shout out for help.

However, where it is not possible to avoid being bound, you will improve your chances of escape significantly if you entice your captor to do the job inadequately. In this section I will cover escapes from being gagged, tied to a chair and having your hands tied, both from the front and the rear. Practise these escapes carefully until you are able to deal with them adequately. All of the skills taught in this section rely on you positioning yourself so that your captor binds you ineffectively. Accordingly, you must not give him any indication about what you are doing or you will put him on his guard. Finally, try pleading with your captor not to tie you up too tightly. It could work!

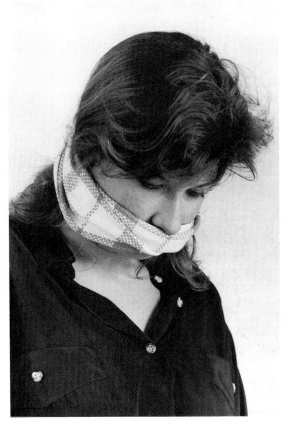

ESCAPE FROM A GAG

1. As the gag is being applied, blow your cheeks out and hold your lips tightly together and, at the same time, clench your teeth to prevent the gag from actually going into your mouth. This will enlarge your face and will make it easier for you to remove the gag.
2. Tuck your chin hard into your chest, which will make the gag that much more difficult to apply (fig. 104).
3. If it is possible, you should stand while the gag is being fitted, as this will make it more difficult for your captor to secure it tightly because he won't have the same amount of leverage to assist him. If you are standing, try not to be too rigid as this will also make it more difficult for him.
4. When you judge it to be safe to attempt to remove the gag, you should deflate your cheeks and relax your face and neck generally. This will give you room to remove it or to slide it down from your mouth.

Fig. 104

ESCAPE FROM BEING TIED TO A CHAIR

1. Position yourself so that you are sitting forwards near the edge of the chair and curve your back to disguise your posture so that your back is resting against the back of the chair. Inhale and extend your stomach to increase the distance from your front to the back of the chair. It will also help if you lean forwards while you are being tied (fig. 105).
2. Push your elbows outwards if your hands are being tied behind your back, and, if your feet are also being tied, keep your knees apart and your ankles crossed (fig. 106).
3. To escape, exhale and hold your stomach in, while at the same time slide back on the seat of the chair. Bring your elbows and knees together and uncross your ankles. Wriggle and try either to remove the ropes or slide out of them.

Figs 105, 106

ESCAPE FROM HAVING YOUR HANDS TIED IN FRONT OF YOU

1. As your hands are being tied together, keep your elbows bent with your wrists as close to your upper body as your captor will allow and offer your wrists at an angle to each other in such a way that there is space between them, even though your hands are firmly together (fig. 107).
2. Tighten all muscles in your arms and wrists as this will increase their overall size.
3. Try to be seated when your hands are being tied as this will make it more difficult for your captor to secure the rope properly.
4. To escape, straighten your elbows and lower your arms, bringing your wrists as close together as possible. Relax the muscles in your arms and wrists. Wriggle and try either to remove the ropes or slide out of them.

Fig. 107

ESCAPE FROM HAVING YOUR HANDS TIED BEHIND YOUR BACK

1. Offer your wrists in a straight line and never crossed. This will help prevent your captor using a cross tie which would be much more difficult to escape from. Try to position your wrists near to the small of your back and bend your body forward as you are being tied. This will cause your wrists to part (fig. 108).
2. Tighten all muscles in your arms and wrists as this will increase their overall size.
3. To escape, straighten your elbows and lower your arms and bring your wrists as close together as possible. Relax the muscles in your arms and wrists. Wriggle and try either to remove the ropes or slide out of them.

Fig. 108

■ ■ Defences Against Strangles and Headlocks ■ ■

Please remember that you should, where possible, already be in the *active stance* when facing these attacks.

DEFENCE AGAINST A TWO-HANDED FRONT STRANGLE

Attack

You have been pushed with your back against a wall and your assailant is strangling you by placing both of his hands round your neck. He is using his weight to add pressure to the strangle (fig. 108).

Fig. 109

Defence 1

1. Starting with both of your arms by your side, raise your left arm in between your assailant's arms and, in an anti-clockwise motion, encircle your assailant's right arm in a complete circle. Continue this circular movement until your left arm is near your own right shoulder. Your assailant's right arm should now be trapped by your left arm and his right elbow will be held in a painful lock by pulling upwards with your left arm (fig. 110).

2. With the heel of your right hand, strike your assailant under his chin. Maintain the pressure on his right arm by continuing to pull upwards with your left arm (fig. 111).

3. With your right leg, reach behind your assailant's legs and throw him backwards by sweeping his legs with yours. Assist the throw by pushing his head backwards with your right hand. As you are throwing him, maintain the pressure on his right arm (fig. 112).

Figs 110, 111, 112

Figs 113, 114

Defence 2

1. Place the palm of your right hand on the back of your assailant's neck while at the same time raise your left arm in between your assailant's arms, so that your fingers are pointing upwards (fig. 113).
2. Stepping to your right, knock your assailant's outstretched right arm out of the way with a sharp chopping action against his elbow with your left arm. Follow this by placing your left hand on the back of his neck. Drive your assailant's head sharply forward with both hands, driving his face into the wall (fig. 114).
3. By turning your head and shoulders to your left while applying this technique, you will find it easy to drive your assailant's head into the wall close to where your own head was originally.

DEFENCE AGAINST A FRONT STRANGLE

Attack

Your assailant has grabbed your throat with his right hand and is attempting to strangle you.

Defence 1

1. Place your left hand on top of your assailant's right wrist, with your thumb near his knuckles and your fingers round the edge (fig. 115).
2. Twist your assailant's hand in an anti-clockwise rotation and, at the same time, bend your assailant's wrist into itself and push sharply downwards with your thumb (fig. 116).
3. Place your right hand in the corresponding position on your assailant's hand (fig. 117).
4. Pull his wrist close to your stomach and step back with your left foot. By continuing with this pushing action with both of your thumbs against the back of his hand, you should be able to force your assailant to the ground, as well as maintaining a very painful wrist lock (fig. 118).

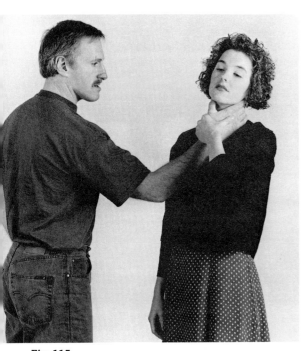

Fig. 115

Figs 116, 117, 118

Defence 2

1. Place your right hand on your assailant's hand, so that your thumb is on the back of his hand and your fingers are round the edge (fig. 119).
2. Push your left hand sharply against his elbow (fig. 120).
3. At the same time as pushing with your left hand, peel your assailant's hand from your throat by rotating your right hand clockwise and bend your assailant's wrist into itself, by pushing hard with your thumb (fig. 121).
4. By continuing the pushing and twisting movements, force your assailant to the ground and maintain both the armlock and the wrist lock.

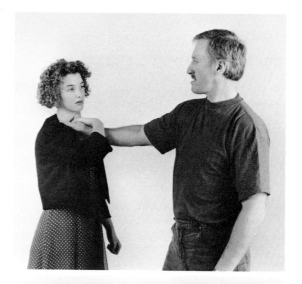

Figs 119, 120, 121

DEFENCE AGAINST A HEADLOCK

Attack

Your assailant has grabbed you in a headlock with his right arm (fig. 122).

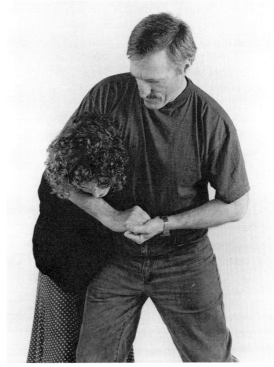

Fig. 122

Defence

1. With the heel of your right hand, sharply strike your assailant's groin (fig. 123).

Fig. 123

2. With the same hand, reach between his legs and grab his trouser leg near the inside of his right thigh (fig. 124).
3. Place your left hand on the side of his face, and force his head backwards and towards his rear left-hand side (fig. 125).
4. Stretch out with your left leg so that it is behind his legs and push your assailant over it by continuing to push with your left hand against his face (fig. 126).

Figs 124, 125, 126

DEFENCE AGAINST A REAR CHOKE

Attack

You are attacked from behind by your assailant placing his right forearm across your throat and he is attempting to choke you.

Defence

This is an extremely dangerous attack which needs to be dealt with quickly, as it can lead to unconsciousness.

1. With your left arm, reach across your own throat and grab hold of your assailant's right arm just above his elbow, while at the same time raise your right arm and grab his arm just below his shoulder. With both of your hands, sharply pull your assailant's arm forwards and downwards. As well as preparing for the defence, this movement will also give you more room to breathe (fig. 127).

2. While continuing with this forwards and downwards pulling action, step well back with your right leg, placing it on the outside of your assailant's right leg, and bend your right knee so that it is about twelve inches off the ground. Bend your body sharply forwards and continue your pulling action and you will be able to throw your assailant over your right shoulder and leg by driving your own head and shoulders downwards towards your left foot. To assist the throw, straighten your right leg as the throw commences (fig. 128).

Fig. 127

Fig. 128

■ ■ ■ ■ ■ Restraining Techniques ■ ■ ■ ■ ■

The techniques taught in this section are designed to restrain an assailant and, ideally, they should be applied quickly and before the assailant resists. This will enable you to effect them more easily. If possible, you should restrain aggression before it starts or at the earliest possible opportunity.

GOOSENECK WRIST LOCK

1. Approaching the assailant from behind (see page 78) and close to his right side, take hold of his right wrist with your right hand, so that your fingers are on the back of his hand and your thumb is on his palm. Grasp his elbow with your left hand (fig. 129).

Figs 129, 130   **Figs 131, 132**

2. Pull his wrist back and upwards towards you and at the same time push his elbow forwards with your left hand. This will apply pressure to his arm and could be sufficient to control him (fig. 130).

3. If you need more control, the technique can be continued by passing your left hand under his right armpit and pushing his right arm forwards and upwards so that his forearm is almost vertical. Ensure that you maintain the same position with your fingers on his right wrist (fig. 131).

4. Press his wrist in on itself by applying pressure with both your fingers and your own wrist and place your left hand in the corresponding position on his wrist. Your assailant's elbow should be trapped against your stomach (fig. 132).

5. Apply the wrist lock by sharply pressing his wrist in on itself with both hands.

DEFENCE TO ASSIST A THIRD PARTY

Attack

This defence can be used against an assailant who is attacking another person. It can also be used to defend yourself if you are able to get behind your assailant (see page 78).

Defence

1. Approaching the assailant from behind, place your right wrist under his chin with the palm of your hand facing downwards and, by lifting your right wrist, force his head backwards and towards his right side (fig. 133).

2. Simultaneously, place your left arm round the outside of his left arm in a hooking motion, trapping his arm. Clench your left fist and force it into the small of his back (fig. 134).

3. By pulling his head backwards with your right hand and pushing his hips forward with your left fist, you will cause him to be off-balance and under your control.

4. You will now be able to propel him forwards or backwards with ease.

Figs 133, 134

HOW TO MOVE BEHIND AN ASSAILANT

This technique demonstrates the principle of moving behind an assailant in order to restrain him. For the purpose of this demonstration, I will show this technique as a defence against an assailant who is threatening to strike you with an object that he is holding in his right hand. *Please note that this technique should not be used where the assailant is brandishing a knife* (fig. 135).

1. Step forward with your left foot and at the same time grab your assailant's attacking right wrist with your left hand. Place your right hand on the back of his right elbow, reaching it from the top, in such a way that your fingers are facing downwards (fig. 136).

2. With a sharp movement, pull the assailant diagonally forwards, using your right arm in such a way that his right foot moves in front of your right foot. Simultaneously, push his right wrist with your left hand and this will apply pressure to his elbow (fig. 137).

3. With your left hand, push his right arm down and step behind him, placing your left forearm across his throat, while keeping hold of his elbow with your right hand. You will find it more effective if you use the bony edge of your forearm rather than the back of it which is more fleshy (fig. 138).

4. As soon as your arm is in position across his throat, pull him sharply backwards towards you and squeeze his neck with your forearm. Ensure that you use your *forearm* to choke the assailant and not the crook of your elbow, as this will allow him too much freedom. Now bring your right hand into position by grabbing hold of your own left hand and use both hands to increase the pressure on the assailant's neck and continue to pull him backwards towards you (fig. 139).

Please note that this technique will incapacitate the assailant as soon as it is applied. If the pressure is maintained on his neck, it will lead to him losing consciousness and even death. Therefore, as soon as this technique has succeeded, slacken the pressure on his neck while keeping your hands in position so that you can re-apply it if necessary.

Figs 135, 136, 137

Fig. 138

Fig. 139

Defences Against Attacks Connected With a Motor Vehicle

This section deals with defences against incidents that can occur while you are in, or are about to enter a motor vehicle.

The majority of confrontations occur as a result of drivers becoming aggressive with each other following an incident that very often is of a trivial nature. Most of these incidents can be prevented altogether simply by not becoming involved in verbal and gesticulatory exchanges with your fellow motorists, no matter how bad you consider their driving to be. Remember too that the horn should not be used aggressively, as this can also lead to unnecessary confrontations.

The defences in this section cover situations where you are attacked as you are entering your car, as well as defences to deal with being assaulted while in the car, either by someone else who is in the vehicle with you, or by someone who

attempts to force your door open to attack you.

If you are driving when the attack occurs, you must decide whether you consider it to be safer to stop the car or to continue driving. Stopping the vehicle has the advantage of enabling you to defend yourself more efficiently, as you will be able to concentrate more fully and you will have the use of your hands and legs; whereas continuing to drive could have the advantage of deterring the assailant, as any aggressive action may cause an accident. It also offers you the opportunity of driving towards a place where you can find help, such as a police station or a well-populated area, or of signalling to other motorists or a passing police car. The correct course of action, therefore, depends very much on the circumstances.

The same principles apply to similar situations, such as when seated in a cinema or on a bus.

Figs 140, 141, 142   **Fig. 143**

DEFENCE AGAINST BEING ATTACKED WHEN YOU ARE ENTERING YOUR CAR

Attack

You are attacked from behind as you are about to enter your car. Your assailant has put his right hand across your mouth (fig. 140).

Defence

1. Bend your left arm, and with your left elbow, strike your assailant hard in his solar plexus (fig. 140).
2. With a clenched left fist, strike your assailant first in his groin and then in his face (figs. 142 & 143). (*It is important to strike him in the groin first, because this will have the effect of causing him to bend his body forward, therefore making the second strike to his face much easier.*)
3. You should now be able to make your escape.

DEFENCE AGAINST AN ATTACK BY A FRONT-SEAT PASSENGER

Attack

Your assailant attempts to grab you with his right hand (fig. 144).

Defence

1. Raise your left arm and sweep his right hand out of the way by moving your arm from left to right (fig. 145).
2. With your right hand, grab hold of his clothing near to his right lapel and pull him sharply towards you in a downwards movement, keeping your left arm against his right arm until you have secured this move (fig. 146).
3. With your left hand, push the back of his head forwards and under your own right arm. You will need to move your right arm so as to make room for his head to pass underneath it. Keep a tight hold on his lapel with your right hand (fig. 147).
4. Reach over his right shoulder with your left hand and push your arm as far forward as possible (fig. 148).
5. You will be able to strangle your assailant by pulling his head backwards and towards you with your right hand whilst continuing to push your left hand forward.

Figs. 144, 145   **Figs 146, 147, 148**

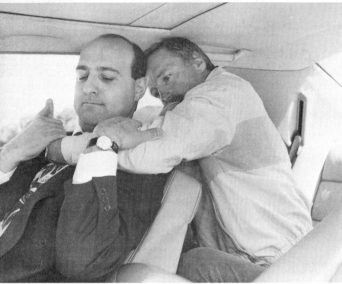

DEFENCE AGAINST AN ATTACK FROM A REAR-SEAT PASSENGER

Attack

Your assailant attempts to strangle you by placing his left arm round your neck (fig. 149).

Defence

1. Tighten your neck muscles and raise your shoulders to help prevent strangulation.
2. With both hands, grab hold of his forearm and pull it sharply forwards and downwards. This will loosen the strangle as well as assist you with this defence (fig. 150).
3. Lower your chin and bite his arm as hard as you can, aiming, if possible, for the fleshy part of his arm (fig. 151).

Figs 149, 150, 151

DEFENCE AGAINST AN ASSAILANT WHO ATTEMPTS TO FORCE YOUR CAR DOOR OPEN TO ATTACK YOU

Attack

Your assailant has managed to open your car door and is about to assault you.

Defence

1. If you are unable to keep the door closed or drive away safely, push the door hard, striking your assailant as fiercely as you can (fig. 152).
2. You should now be able to retake control of the door by grabbing it and then closing it ·firmly and locking it. Drive away as soon as you safely can.
3. It is important to apply the second movement as soon as your assailant has been stunned by the first move. Do not allow him time to recover.

Fig. 152

■ ■ ■ Defences Against Weapon Attacks ■ ■ ■

Please remember that you should, where possible, already be in the *active stance* when facing these attacks.

In this section, I will deal with defences against weapon attacks. Please remember that weapons can and often do kill. **You must always consider surrendering whenever a weapon is used, unless you believe that doing so will place you in greater danger.** This is by no means a cowardly reaction. Your possessions can be replaced – your life can not.

It is, of course, possible that an assailant will not offer you the opportunity of surrender. He could actually *attack* you with a weapon, rather than just *threaten* you with one. In these circumstances, the techniques shown in this section could prove to be invaluable. I have, therefore, deliberately avoided teaching a wide selection of defences in this section and have concentrated on a few very basic techniques that can be used effectively by people without a great deal of experience.

Some teaching material also demonstrates defences to attacks with firearms. I have inten-tionally omitted dealing with any physical defences to such attacks, as the only sensible option you have, apart from the use of the non-physical advice given in this book, is to surrender.

When faced with deadly weapons such as firearms, you *must* surrender. The following advice will be useful in such situations:

- Try and stay calm. Your calmness and composure could also extend to others, including the gunman. He will be in a desperate frame of mind and will probably not know what he wants to do.
- Say nothing and do nothing unless you are told to by the gunman. The only exception is where you feel that you are able to calm him down. Remember that he will be extremely tense and will probably lack confidence.
- Do as you are told. Do not argue.
- Do not try to disarm him. Remember that it only takes a minute movement for the trigger to be activated.
- Appear friendly and if you do converse with him, never patronize or belittle him.

DEFENCE AGAINST A KNIFE

Attack

Your assailant is threatening you with a knife which he is holding in his right hand.

Defence 1

1. Step back out of your assailant's reach and remove your coat or other heavy garment. Wrap it round your left arm and use this arm to parry any attacks made by your assailant. Take up the active stance shown earlier, with your left arm and leg leading, thus greatly reducing the target area (fig. 153).

2. As your assailant lunges at you, move out of the way to avoid the attack and deflect it as necessary with your protected left arm. At the same time, kick him as hard as you can in his groin with your right foot, remembering to snap your foot back as soon as the kick has been delivered, to prevent him from catching hold of your leg. The force of this kick should cause his upper body to bend forward (fig. 154).

3. Grab his head with both hands and force it downwards. Raise your right knee and drive it hard into his face, while continuing to drive his head down with your hands (fig. 155).

4. You should now be able to make your escape.

Figs 153, 154, 155

Defence 2

1. With a clapping action, clap your assailant's outstretched arm, so that your left hand claps his wrist and your right hand claps his forearm. Make this clap as sharp and as forceful as you can (fig. 156).
2. This action should cause your assailant's hand to open and the knife to drop. If you can make a safe escape, you must do so immediately.
3. If you are unable to escape, do not attempt to pick the knife up. If your assailant bends down to retrieve it, his head and face could be in a vulnerable position, which will enable you to kick him hard in his face and then make your escape.

Fig. 156

DEFENCE AGAINST A STRIKE WITH A BATON

Attack

Your assailant attempts to hit you on the head with a baton which he is holding in his right hand.

Defence 1

1. Step slightly to the left, so that you are not directly underneath the weapon should your assailant drop it during your defence. Raise both of your arms diagonally in the shape of a cross and block the attack by trapping your assailant's forearm between your own crossed forearms. This blocking action should be carried out with as much force as possible. Step forward with your left leg during this move, and bend your left knee. This will result in his elbow bending. It will also have the effect of reducing much of the force of the attack (fig. 157).

Fig. 157

2. Grab your assailant's right wrist with your right hand and at the same time move your left arm underneath and behind his right arm and grab your own right wrist in such a way that your left palm is facing your assailant (fig. 158).

3. You are now in a good position to apply an entangled armlock on your assailant, as follows:

   i) Bend your right wrist forward, as if you were revving a motor-bike, and at the same time straighten your right arm in front of you.

   ii) Tilt your left forearm by pushing your left wrist forward and moving your left elbow towards yourself (fig. 159).

4. Step forward with your left leg and place your left foot on the ground to the outside rear of his right leg. Then, step forward with your right leg and, moving it behind his legs, place it on the ground behind his legs and throw him backwards by pushing with your arms which are still maintaining the armlock. You may find it helpful to sweep your right leg backwards into his legs to assist with the throw (fig. 160).

Fig. 158   **Figs 159, 160**

Defence 2

1. Step slightly to the left, so that you are not directly underneath the weapon should your assailant drop it during your defence. Raise both of your arms diagonally in the shape of a cross and block the attack by trapping your assailant's forearm between your own crossed forearms. This blocking action should be carried out with as much force as possible. Step forward with your left leg during this move, and bend your left knee. This will have the effect of reducing much of the force of the attack (see fig. 157 on p. 85).

2. Grab your assailant's right wrist with your right hand and pull his right arm tightly across your chest. Ensure that the outside of his elbow is near your chest and that his knuckles are facing you (fig. 161).

3. With the heel of your left hand, strike your assailant under his chin and push his head away from you (fig. 162).

4. With your left leg, step behind his legs and continue to push his head with your left hand, and push him backwards over your left knee (fig. 163).

Figs 161, 162, 163

■ ■ ■ ■ ■ Defences on the Ground ■ ■ ■ ■ ■

This section deals with situations where your assailant (and maybe you as well) are on the ground.

There are many situations where you can end up in this position and many assailants will attempt to pin you there while carrying out their attack. It could be that you have managed to put your assailant on the ground and you feel that you need to apply further techniques in order to assure your own safety. You could also be in this position because you were lying down when you were attacked (for example in bed or sunbathing) or, through struggling with your assailant, you have ended up there. Your assailant could be straddling you, perhaps with your arms trapped. He could be attempting to rape you. Whatever the position or reason, the techniques in this section deal with these situations.

The techniques taught in this section are particularly relevant to rape and other forms of sexual assault as they would normally occur on the ground. They can, of course, be used just as effectively against a mugger as they can against these types of attack.

DEFENCE AGAINST BEING HELD DOWN

Attack

You are on your back and your assailant is on top of you. He could be trying to remove your clothing.

Defence 1

This technique may not appear to be powerful, but you can be assured that it is. If you still need convincing, try it on yourself first. **But do so very gently. It can cause severe pain and damage.**

1. 'Cup' both of your hands and simultaneously slap both of your assailant's ears with as much force as you can manage. Keep your fingers close together when applying this technique (fig. 164).

Fig. 164

Defence 2 (assailant grabbing your throat with his right hand)

1. Raise your left arm and place it on top of your assailant's right forearm, trapping it against your chest. Ensure that you force his forearm tightly against your chest (fig. 165).
2. Strike him under his chin with a palm fist using your right hand. Ensure that you keep his right forearm pinned tightly to your chest (fig. 166).
3. By continuing to push with your right palm fist, you will be able to force your assailant off you.

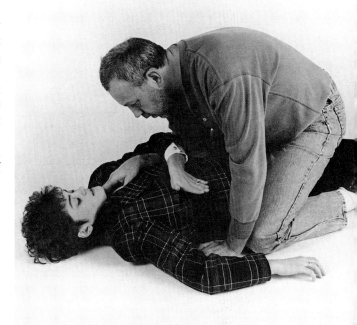

Figs 165, 166

Defence 3 (assailant grabbing your throat with his right hand)

1. Grab your assailant's right wrist with your right hand and at the same time place your left hand on the outside of his right elbow. With your left hand, push his elbow towards the ground near to your right shoulder, making sure that you keep your right hand on his right wrist. Bend your left knee and place your left foot firmly on the ground (fig. 167).

2. Continue to force his right arm towards the ground and, using your left foot as leverage, roll towards your right side, forcing your assailant off you, while maintaining the armlock that you have applied with your left hand (fig. 168).

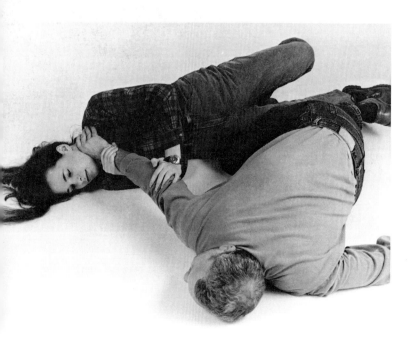

Figs 167, 168

Defence 4 (assailant has trapped both of your hands)

1. Raise both knees and smash them as hard as you can into his buttocks, forcing him to shoot forwards (fig. 169).

2. At the same time as his body is being propelled forwards, turn your own body sharply onto one side and strike him as hard as you can in his groin, using a palm fist. Then, grab his testicles, and squeeze, twist and pull them as hard as you can (fig. 170).

3. Force him off you while maintaining your grip on his testicles. Keep squeezing, twisting and pulling until you are standing up and you can escape.

Don't be squeamish about this. Remember your life is in danger. You must do whatever is necessary to escape.

Figs 169, 170

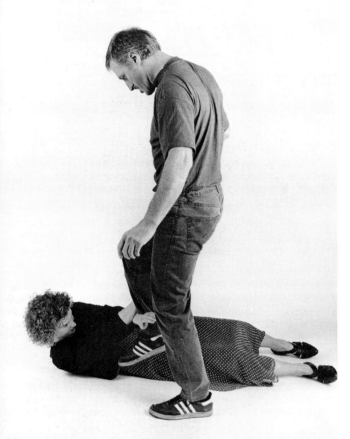

DEFENCE AGAINST A KICK

Attack

You are on your back and your assailant attempts to kick you.

Defence

1. Roll towards your assailant and block the kick by forming a cross with your forearms (fig. 171).
2. Raise your upper leg and place it across and in front of his hips, so that your foot rests on his stomach. At the same time, place your lower leg just above and behind his ankles. Using a scissor action, sharply sweep your assailant's body with both legs, throwing him backwards to the ground (fig. 172).

Figs 171, 172

DEFENCE AGAINST A RAPE ATTACK

Attack

Your assailant is on top of you and is attempting to rape you. He also has his right hand across your throat and is attempting to strangle you.

Defence

This is an extremely dangerous attack which needs to be dealt with quickly, as it can lead to unconsciousness.

1. Place both of your hands on your assailant's hand (as shown) and try to ease the pressure on your throat by pulling his hand away from you. You will not be able to break his grip on your throat (fig. 173).
2. Raise your left leg over your assailant's head and bring it in front of his throat. Your knee should be slightly bent. Force him to your left side with your outstretched left leg (fig. 174).
3. Continue to push him with your left leg until his back is on the ground and your leg is across his throat. Pull his right arm towards you and move your hips in towards him so that there is no gap in between his shoulder and your groin and that his elbow is across your hips. Keep pressing down with your left leg and at the same time lift your hips off the ground and pull his right arm sharply down. Keep his outstretched right hand as close to your throat as possible and you will have secured a very painful armlock (fig. 175).

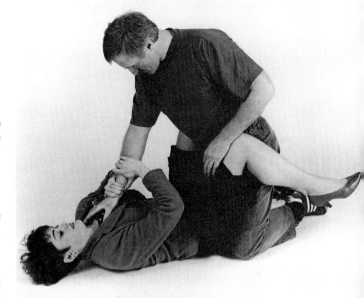

Figs 173, 174, 175

DEFENCE AGAINST A STRANGLE

Attack

You are lying on your back and your assailant is on top of you. He is attempting to strangle you with both of his hands around your throat. His arms are straight (fig. 176).

Defence 1

This is an extremely dangerous attack which needs to be dealt with quickly, as it can lead to unconsciousness.

1. Starting with both of your arms by your side, hook your assailant's right arm with your left arm and place it in between his arms, thus encircling his right arm. Continue this circular movement until your left arm is near your own right shoulder. Your assailant's right arm should now be trapped by your left arm and his right elbow should be held in a painful lock by pulling upwards and against his elbow joint with your left arm (fig. 177).
2. Bend your right knee and place your right foot firmly on the ground. At the same time, using your right foot as leverage, roll towards your left side (fig. 178).
3. Grab your assailant's throat with your right hand and push hard. Do not release the pressure on the armlock (fig. 179).
4. You should now be able to push your assailant off you and stand up. Maintain the pressure on the armlock until you are satisfied of your safety (fig. 180).

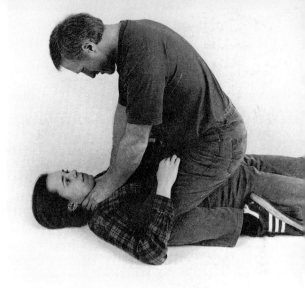

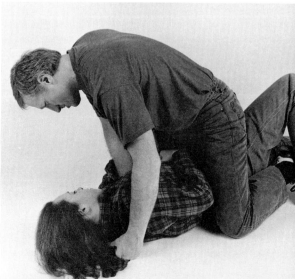

Figs 176, 177, 178

Defence 2 (assailant's arms are bent)

1. Press both of your thumbs hard into your assailant's eyes. If he is wearing spectacles, first knock them off. You may find that you can apply more pressure with your thumbs if you grip the sides of his head with your fingers. For greatest effect, you should use the tips of your thumbs for this technique.
2. Continue to press his eyes and you should be able to drive his head backwards, forcing him off you (fig. 181).

Figs 179, 180

Fig. 181

■ ■ ■ Groundwork Restraining Techniques ■ ■ ■

This section deals with situations where you and your assailant are on the ground and you need to control and restrain him. These techniques differ from those in the previous section, in that they are intended to *control and restrain* your assailant, who, because of the intensity of his violence, needs to be kept under control, either until help arrives or the situation changes.

It could be that you have judged the situation to be too dangerous to allow him to get up, or that if you tried to make your escape you would be in grave danger.

Your assailant will probably be struggling vigorously as you are holding him. You should move your body with his and try to maintain the same relative body positions.

SCARF HOLD

This technique is so called because you are controlling your assailant by wrapping your arms round his neck and shoulders like a scarf (fig. 182).

1. Circle your right arm around your assailant's neck and grip your own clothing near to your own chest.
2. Trap his right arm under your left armpit and take hold of his forearm, pulling as tightly as

possible. Lower your head and spread your legs so as to maintain good balance.

3. Raise your right arm slightly from the ground to squeeze your assailant's neck, so that his shoulders are raised from the ground. This will have the effect of making it difficult for him to breathe.

   Great care must be taken with this step. You should only apply pressure sufficient to control your assailant and not to stop him from breathing.

Fig. 182

UPPER-BODY HOLD

This hold-down is particularly useful where your assailant is in a position where his head is nearest to you and his legs are pointing away (fig. 183).

1. Place your body on top of your assailant's body, so that your chest is over his, and your head is pointing towards his feet.
2. Bend your arms and grab hold of his clothing near to each side of his waist, pushing your elbows into his armpits at the same time.
3. Spread your legs wide apart to improve your stability and by bending your toes back, press downwards with the balls of your feet.
4. Alternatively, instead of spreading your legs as shown above, you could bring both of your knees up towards your assailant and place them as close to him as possible, again pressing down on the ground with the balls of your feet to improve your stability.

Fig. 183

ENTANGLED ARMLOCK

1. Leaning across your assailant's body, grab his left wrist with your left hand, bending his elbow at 90 degrees with his palm facing upwards. Force his back flat on to the ground with your chest (fig. 184).
2. Slide your right hand under his upper arm and take hold of your own left wrist in such a way that the palm of your right hand is facing downwards (fig. 185).
3. Bend your left wrist downwards as though you were revving a motor-bike, ensuring that you keep your hands as close to the ground as possible (fig. 186).
4. With your right elbow, lever his elbow from the ground and you will have applied the entangled armlock (fig. 187).
5. By stretching one of your legs backwards, you will increase the pressure on his chest and be able to apply more leverage to the armlock.

Fig. 184

Figs 185, 186, 187

■ ■ ■ ■ Rape and Other Sexual Assaults ■ ■ ■ ■

As you will have noted from the earlier sections, if you are ever unfortunate enough to come face-to-face with a mugger, you could well have the option of giving up whatever the assailant has demanded.

In a sexually motivated attack, the option of surrender poses significant danger. Recent research has suggested that in cases where the assailant is unknown to their victim, those victims who fight back actually *double* their chances of not being raped or seriously sexually assaulted and do not significantly increase their levels of injury. Therefore, in contrast to the myth that the rapist always succeeds, the evidence indicates that approximately 70 per cent of the women who fight back actually avoid being raped. I have repeated this information here because it is crucial that you fully recognise the significance of the distinction between the two types of assault outlined.

I am afraid that if you are ever unfortunate enough to be faced with such an awesome predic-ament then you must decide for yourself, and quickly, how you are going to respond. However, it is undeniable that the more proficient and confi-dent you become in self defence, the better your chances will be, no matter what decision you take.

Of course, you do have the option to submit – to give in to the attack and do as the assailant demands. Although this is not an attractive option, submission could be the *only* way to halt the physical attack. If you do feel that submission is your best chance of survival, you should still be looking for any possible openings for an escape or counter-attack. In these circumstances, you must never consider that you have *consented* to the attack. Submitting and consenting are fundamen-tally different. When someone *consents* to sex, that person wants to participate, whereas when someone submits, the victim believes there is no other option.

In about half of the reported cases involving sexual assault, the attacker is known to the victim. Some women think that, because they know who their attacker is, the police will assume that they, in some way, consented to the attack. This fear, however, is simply not justified.

In the case of rape, you are urged to report the attack to the police as soon as possible. Do not bathe or change your clothing until you have been examined, as you may destroy vital evidence leading to the conviction of the rapist. Do not drink any alcohol or take any medication until you have made your statement to the police. You will be treated very sympathetically and the police will endeavour to have you examined by a woman doctor. You will also receive advice about post-coital birth control and you can be referred to a clinic specializing in sexually transmitted diseases. You would be well advised to take the advice of the police and the examining doctor. It is far better in these circumstances to be safe rather than sorry. Some useful contact names are listed at the end of this book.

I have also included a section dealing with physical self-defence techniques that can be used in the event of rape or other types of sexual assault. You will find this section starting at page 88. Please read the entire physical self-defence section, as many of the later techniques will require you to have grasped the principles shown earlier.

> '*I didn't report the attack to the police because I was ashamed. Then I heard that he had raped another woman. I feel sick thinking that my silence allowed this animal to do it again.*'

∎ ∎ ∎ ∎ Be Alert, Safe and Streetwise ∎ ∎ ∎ ∎

Alertness is being switched on to what is happening around you. Alertness is a state of mind. In the context of self defence, it is a state of mind where observation should be so automatic it is almost subconscious. It must be achieved without effort. Alertness should only be brought into a more conscious state when danger is either detected or suspected. Safety and alertness can be learned, so that they are almost second nature. They should co-exist. With these skills, you will know how to avoid an unpleasant situation before it is too late.

When you fasten your seat belt in the car, you are clearly *not* saying 'I'm going to be involved in a traffic accident today.' All you are doing is preparing yourself just *in case* something happens. Neither would you consider *not* wearing your seat belt just because *you* are a good driver; how about the unpredictable behaviour of others? In self-defence terms, it is exactly the same. You must cultivate a higher level of awareness which, just as in the examples above, is casual and doesn't intrude on your everyday life.

The alert car driver, seeing an accident ahead, takes note of the potential danger and is able to avoid crashing into the debris. A driver who is inattentive, however, could well end up being involved in the accident himself. Similarly, in self-defence terms, an alert person who sees a gang of youths harassing others will take the necessary action to avoid them, whereas his inattentive counterpart will walk straight into danger.

Once you have developed a better understanding of the skills needed to enhance your levels of awareness, you will find that they will become second nature and instinctive. You will then be in an excellent position to utilize these skills to avoid areas of potential risk and danger. Beware of alcohol and drugs and of becoming over-tired, as these will all have an adverse effect on your ability to be aware of danger.

Consider the following situations: You are alone at home and, late one night, someone rings your doorbell; or, you are walking home and you think that someone is following you; or, maybe you have been offered a lift home from a party by a stranger. All of these everyday situations require you to be alert to the possibility of danger.

Think for a moment about the senses that are required for everyday situations: crossing the road, driving a car, cooking a meal, climbing a ladder. They all require a certain degree of what we might call 'common sense'. This so-called common sense comes from years of experience. To illustrate the point, a young child would have great difficulty in carrying out these simple tasks, but as the child gets older, it would be able to perform them with greater dexterity.

In the next section, I will illustrate some useful examples of how better observation and awareness skills can be of immense benefit to you. I hope that you will allocate some time to consider the section carefully and think about your own everyday life and how you can enhance your own safety.

Remember, avoiding any dangerous situation must always be your best option.

∎ ∎ ∎ ∎ Essential Advice on Safety ∎ ∎ ∎ ∎

ON THE STREET

Being vigilant on the street is one of the most important aspects of your personal safety. Great care must be taken, particularly when you are out alone or after dark. You should avoid, at all cost, walking in deserted unlit areas and subways, even if it is a short-cut home. Instead, keep to main roads with pavements that are busy and well lit, or better still, arrange to be collected. If you walk home or go jogging or cycling on a regular basis, try to vary your route and time, so that you do not give an assailant any indication about your journey patterns.

Have you ever walked past someone only to fear that they might decide to follow you? To turn your head might provoke the other person, although to ignore the possibility could prove to be dangerous. If you think that you are being followed, reflections and shadows can be of great assistance to you. Think of anything that is reflective, such as a shop window or the glass in a telephone booth. Looking at the ground can often reveal shadows, too. If this is not possible, then cross the road, looking left and right before you do so. Take advantage of this normal road safety procedure to observe the situation discreetly.

The following list will help keep you and your family safe when out on the street:

- Do not take short-cuts home and avoid deserted unlit areas and subways.
- Always walk in the middle of the pavement as this will help prevent being grabbed by someone lurking in doorways, bushes or alleys.
- Do not have expensive-looking jewellery on show. Cover it up.
- Do not hitch-hike or accept lifts from strangers.
- Always walk facing on-coming traffic to avoid a vehicle sneaking up from behind you.
- If you should be threatened by the occupants of a car that does stop near you, scream loudly and run in the opposite direction to that which the car is facing.
- Keep your hands as free as possible and out of your pockets.
- Carry your bag close to your body and always consider giving it up if someone grabs it. Just in case, carry your keys, cheque book and credit cards in your pocket and divide your cash into different pockets.
- Don't make it easy for pickpockets. Carry your wallet or purse in an inside pocket if at all possible.
- Leave your personal stereo at home – wearing one will reduce your ability to hear footsteps or other movements.
- Arrange to be collected if you are out late, or take a taxi. Always ask the driver to wait until you are inside your house safely.
- Don't have your back to potential danger when using cash dispensers or payphones. Wherever possible, face the street and continually scan the area for signs of danger. Do not place your bag or purse on top of the equipment or between your legs as it can easily be snatched.
- Carry a personal attack alarm to scare off an assailant, particularly if you are regularly out late or have to walk through isolated areas.
- If you walk, jog or cycle on a regular basis, vary your route and time.
- If you think that you are being followed, cross the road and see if the other person follows. If he does, and you are certain that it is not just a coincidence, run to the nearest busy place and call the police. Scream loudly or sound your personal attack alarm as you are running in an effort to deter him.
- Don't stop walking if a group of people try to stop you and ask you for such things as a match or the time. Continue walking while replying that you don't smoke or haven't got whatever they have requested. This will prevent them from surrounding you and will also show them that you are not intimidated by them.
- Don't ignore anything that you consider *could* mean danger. Assume that it *does* and react accordingly.

I was recently contacted by a delegate who had, some months earlier, attended one of my self-defence courses. She told me about an incident she had been involved in the previous week. She was convinced that, had it not been for the advice given on the course, she would almost certainly have fallen victim to a gang of street muggers.

She was returning home, with her boyfriend, from a night out and, as they turned the corner of her road, she could see a gang of four youths who were partially hidden from view by the wall of an alleyway between some houses. She felt uneasy about walking past them and there was no other way to get to her house and she was already late.

She crossed the road with her boyfriend and they continued to walk towards her house. She put her handbag under her arm and held on to it tightly. She had learned to carry her house keys in her pocket and not to keep all her cash together in one place. Despite feeling afraid, she adopted an upright, assertive and confident walk, and they passed the youths without incident. However, she remained alert to the possibility that they could follow her, but thankfully they did not.

She then heard the sound of scuffling from

where she had earlier seen the youths and, as she turned round, she saw the youths attacking a man and then run off with his briefcase. The entire incident was over in a matter of seconds.

She is convinced that, had she not crossed the road when she did, thereby making it clear to the youths that they had been seen, or presented herself in a less confident way, she would have been their victim instead.

IN THE HOME

Alertness and safety are equally important in the home. Exhibit caution when dealing with unexpected callers, especially at night. Verify their identity before allowing them access. If your front door is solid and denies you the advantage of seeing a caller before opening it, consider fitting a 'spy hole' viewer. A security chain is also useful, so that when you do open the door it will only open a few inches until you release the chain.

If you are alone, you might try calling out 'I'll go, Tom' in a loud voice, to give the caller the impression that there is someone else with you in the house.

Do not open the door (or release the chain) until you are satisfied about the caller's credentials. If the caller claims to be an official, whether a postman, a meter reader or even the police, ask to see his identification. Take your time and examine this identification carefully. Satisfy yourself that it is genuine. If you are still in any doubt, close the door and telephone the appropriate authority to verify the caller's identity.

Never rely on any telephone number given by the caller, even if it is printed on his card, as the number could belong to an accomplice. If you don't have a telephone, or if it is outside normal working hours, tell the caller to come back at another time, after making an appointment through the official channels.

Even if the caller claims that the visit is an emergency, do not be pressurized into allowing him access. He might, for example, claim that there has been an accident and needs to use your telephone. In this situation, you should tell the caller that you will make the call yourself, while he waits outside.

If you are ever in doubt about a caller, summon help or telephone the police. Always remember, you do not have to let anyone into your home if you don't like the look of them. Bogus callers are very often professionals. Do not let them pressurize you into allowing them access. Consider the following example.

A man rings your doorbell late at night and tells you that his car has broken down and asks to use your telephone. Outside it is raining heavily and it is very cold. Imagine the following conversation:

Man: *'My car has broken down. May I come in and use your telephone?'*
Householder: *'If you give me the number, I will make the call for you.'*
Man: *'Look, it's freezing out here and I haven't got a coat. I only want to use your phone. I'll be as quick as I can.'*
Householder: *'I'm sorry. Give me the number and I'll be happy to make the call for you.'*
Man: *'You're being silly now and frankly I'm getting rather annoyed.'*
Householder: *'I'm sorry about that, but I am not going to allow you in the house. If you want to give me the number, I'll make the call for you; if not, goodnight.'*

Despite the freezing weather outside, the householder doesn't know the caller and, notwithstanding her concern, she sticks to her initial decision to refuse him access. Eventually the man will get the message that he will not be allowed into the house.

If you are in any doubt about the necessity of such a refusal – after all he *could* be genuine and totally harmless – don't be. It is absolutely essential for your safety. You must *never* allow such a caller into your house, no matter how much he tries to persuade you, because you can *never* be certain whether he is really genuine or whether he is the nasty exception who correctly puts us all on our guard.

It has been known for confidence tricksters to apply make-up to their faces in an attempt to add authenticity to their ruse. If, as you are reading this, you believe that, if ever faced with such a dilemma, *you* would be able to distinguish the difference between, say, blood and make-up, think again. Just consider how realistic scenes of horrific injury appear in the cinema. *The plain fact is, you* can never be certain of distinguishing the genuine caller from the criminal. If the emergency is genuine, you have offered to call the authorities who will be on the scene within a very short space of time and, similarly, if the incident is not so crucial, for example a car breakdown, then he can quite easily wait outside or in his car.

This example also illustrates the correct use of assertion where, by not fudging the issue of refusing access, the message gets through to the caller and the conversation ends without incident. Note the use of the *Broken Record* technique discussed earlier.

> '*He told me that he had been involved in an accident, so I let him in. How was I to know any different. Once inside, he appeared to change into a totally different person. Even his accent altered. He ended up robbing and raping me.*
> *Now I check on all strangers who call and I always secure my house thoroughly – even if I am only popping next door. I really feel much safer now.* '

If you do allow a caller into your home, take care and stay with him while he is on your premises. Don't leave money or valuables lying around in easy reach. Do not allow him to distract you if he asks you to fetch him something. Do not leave him alone in the room. If he is with a 'colleague', be careful that one of them doesn't keep you talking while the other one burgles your home. This trick is often carried out on your doorstep, so don't be fooled just because you have refused access. Don't hand over money to anyone you don't know. Always remember, if you don't like the look of a caller, don't let him into your house. Don't be afraid or embarrassed to check any caller's identity thoroughly. Genuine callers will recognize the need for these sensible precautions.

A 'personal attack' button linked to your burglar alarm is very helpful in the event of an attack. One alarm button should be situated close to your front door and *at least* one other should be fitted inside the house, for example in the main bedroom. This room should also be designated a 'safe room' and should have strong quality locks fitted to a heavy door. A telephone extension should also be fitted in this bedroom so that help can be summoned quickly if required. If you consider yourself to be particularly at risk, a portable cellular telephone kept in this room would prove to be vital in the event of an intruder cutting your normal telephone wires.

Portable attack alarms that, when activated, let off a deafening siren are also very useful both for home use and when travelling. These should be kept easily to hand so that they can be used without having to spend time trying to locate it. I highly recommend these devices, as an assailant would be discouraged by the deafening shriek emitted, and this could also act to summon help. Because of the importance of these alarms, I have provided further information about them and their use later in this book.

DISCOVERING BURGLARS IN THE NIGHT

Being awoken in the night by noises or footsteps in the house is an unnerving experience. You should not confront the burglar, nor should you lie still, pretending to be asleep, as both of these courses of action are risky. If the burglar thinks that you are asleep, he could decide to move upstairs where you could be in serious danger.

Instead, you should make plenty of noise and turn some lights on. Move about a lot, so that the burglar can hear you. Whether you are alone or not, call out loudly to a male friend, to give the impression that you have male company. All but the most persistent burglars will flee rather than chance a confrontation. Always telephone the police as soon as it is safe to do so. Don't touch anything until the police have made their examination.

RETURNING HOME AND DISCOVERING A BREAK-IN

If, when you are returning home, you find signs of a break-in, never enter the house. It is possible that the intruders could still be inside. Do not let them know that you have arrived home. Go to a neighbour's house or the nearest public telephone and dial 999 to summon the police. If possible, until the police arrive, keep watch on your house from a safe position. If you see the intruders leave, try to get a good description of them and observe which way they go. If they use a vehicle, note down its registration number, make and colour.

Because burglary is one of the most common crimes and its effects can be so devastating to the victim, I have included a section dealing with **Home Security** which can be found on page 107.

WHEN TRAVELLING BY CAR

One of the benefits of travelling by car is the enhanced security that it provides. You will be able to avoid walking home in the dark or worry about catching the last bus or train. However, there are still risks attached to this mode of transport and, although these risks are small, you can improve your personal security by taking some simple precautions. This section shows you how.

When driving, particularly at night or when alone, lock **all** doors and keep **all** windows closed. Ensure that valuables, particularly handbags, purses, wallets and the like, are kept well out of sight, so they do not act as a temptation to any would-be thief. It is also a sensible precaution to lock the boot, particularly if it contains valuables.

When stopping your car at a junction or traffic lights, leave sufficient space in front to manoeuvre and drive away, should you need to do so suddenly. The correct distance is one where you can easily see the bottom of the tyres of the vehicle in front of you. Also, in a situation of danger, engage first gear and keep your right foot near to the accelerator, so that you can drive away hurriedly if the need arises.

It was reported in the national press on Saturday 29 August 1992 that a forty-one-year-old woman was attacked by two men who climbed into her car when she stopped at traffic lights in north London. She was forced, at knife-point, to drive to an unknown location, where she was sexually assaulted. This particular assault occurred in broad daylight in a public place. The advice given above will greatly diminish the possibility of you becoming a victim to such an attack.

Vigilance is also important when you return to your parked car. Be alert to the possibility, no matter how remote, that an intruder has gained access to your vehicle and is hiding inside, awaiting your return. Some years back, there were several reported cases of men stalking car parks and hiding on the floor between the front and rear seats of lone female drivers' cars. They would then pounce on the unsuspecting driver when she returned later to her vehicle.

If at all possible, you should avoid using multistorey car parks, particularly at night. If you can't avoid it, then park on the floor as near to street level as possible, in a well-lit area and close to the ramps or stairs. Better still, park as close as you can to the manned pay booths. When parking in a bay, reverse into the space, so you can leave quickly if necessary.

Take the case of a car driver who is being signalled to stop by what appears to be another motorist in distress. Is this other motorist really in distress, or does he want this driver to stop for other unsavoury reasons? In these circumstances, you should not stop your car. It would be more practical, and of course safer, for you to report the incident at the next available telephone or police station. If you must investigate further, open your window just wide enough to speak to whoever has signalled for you to stop and explain to him that you will go and summon help. Ensure that you keep **all** doors locked and do not allow him into your car. Do not turn off your engine and keep your foot on the accelerator with first gear engaged, in case you need to drive off in a hurry. When stopping, ensure that you leave sufficient space in front of you, to enable you to make a quick escape if it proves necessary.

> ' I got out of my car to try and help. How was I to know it was just a ploy. I will never make that mistake again. '

If you are driving home, and think that you are being followed, do not drive straight home. You might want to satisfy yourself that you are in fact being followed by making several alterations to the journey. If you decide that you are being followed, pull into the left-hand lane and drive slowly. The chances are that the other driver will soon get fed up following you and will drive past.

If not, try to find a busy, well-lit area – a hospital, a petrol filling station or a shopping centre – and stop your car close to other people. Summon help by sounding your horn and flashing your lights. Alternatively, drive to a police station, or if you see a police car, signal for it to stop.

In the sections dealing with the physical self-defence techniques, I have included defences for use in connection with a motor vehicle.

The following useful tips should prove helpful to enhance your safety when travelling by car:

■ Ensure that you have sufficient money with you and enough fuel to complete your journey. Always carry a spare five litres of petrol in a safety can.

■ Before starting off on a long journey, ensure that there is nothing wrong with your car that could cause you to break down. It is a wise precaution to keep your car regularly serviced as, according to RAC figures, over 50 per cent of the breakdowns they attend are caused by a lack of basic car maintenance. Many potentially threatening situations for motorists arise as a result of breakdowns.

■ Plan your route before starting your journey to reduce the likelihood of getting lost. Keep to main roads if possible and carry a map, just in case you get lost. This will avoid your having to ask a stranger for directions.

■ Do not pick up hitch-hikers.

■ Ensure that you have sufficient change and a telephone card, in case you need to make an emergency telephone call. Better still, if you can afford it, have a car telephone fitted or keep a portable telephone with you. Having one, in itself, will greatly enhance your security and peace of mind and could well act as a deterrent to a would-be assailant. You can also buy an imitation car phone, which can also have the same deterrent effect.

■ Carry an emergency puncture repair spray, which could prove invaluable, particularly if your puncture occurs in an isolated area.

■ Before leaving, inform the people at the other end of your estimated time of arrival.

■ Do not be fooled into getting out of your car unless there is an emergency. Ensure that the emergency is real and not a ruse to divert your attention.

■ If, in the event of a breakdown or other emergency, you have cause to stop on the hard-shoulder of a motorway, try to coast to the nearest emergency telephone. Pull up slightly beyond the telephone, so that you are not obscured by your vehicle when making your call and so that you can be seen by passing motorists. These telephones are usually no further than one mile apart. Arrows on marker posts, which are situated at regular intervals along the hard-shoulder, point to the nearest emergency telephone. Telephone the police or breakdown services, and sit on the embankment until they arrive, leaving your vehicle by the passenger door. *One in eight motorway deaths occur on the hard-shoulder, so don't wait in the car.* If you feel at risk from the occupants of another car that pulls up, return to your car via the front passenger door and sit upright in the passenger seat. This will keep you furthest away from the traffic and will also give the impression that your fellow traveller has gone to summon help. Ensure that all windows are closed and doors locked. As soon as you are satisfied that the risk has disappeared, return to the embankment. *Never* accept a lift from a stranger, even to the emergency telephone. If you break down on the motorway and use your car telephone to summon help, repeat the call as soon as possible using one of the emergency telephones as this will pinpoint your *exact* location.

■ If you are involved in an accident and you are at all suspicious about the other driver, do not get out of your car. There is absolutely no requirement for you to do so. Wind down your window just far enough to exchange details.

■ Keep all doors locked when driving and keep the windows closed, particularly in towns. Keep your valuables out of sight and your boot locked.

■ At night, park in a busy, well-lit place. Be vigilant before you get out of the car.

■ When returning to your car, always have your key ready and check that there is no one in the car before entering.

■ When parking in a bay, reverse into the space, so you can leave quickly if necessary.

■ Join a motoring organization.

WHEN TRAVELLING BY PUBLIC TRANSPORT

Travelling late at night on public transport has its own risks attached to it. Where possible, you should choose to sit near to other people, or better still, the driver. Never elect to sit in the upstairs section of a double-deck bus, or in an isolated carriage of a train.

Bus or train stations themselves can be dangerous places. Try and stand in a well-lit area, or near a group of mixed-sex people. Or there may be a manned office that could give you some reassurance. You should avoid standing or being anywhere near disorderly crowds. If such a boisterous and unruly crowd should come in your direction, move.

If after having arrived at your destination you are to be collected, don't wait in a dark, secluded area. A prior arrangement to be met is to be encouraged. Arrange to be met in a well-lit spot or a busy premises, say a chip shop or a taxi office. Always ask your driver to wait until you are in your house safely.

WHEN TRAVELLING BY TAXI

If you need a taxi, you can hail one from the street. Alternatively, you can use a minicab which is only allowed to carry passengers who have made a prior booking. It is a sensible precaution to carry with you the telephone number of a firm you know, so that you have the added comfort of knowing who you are dealing with.

If you need to telephone for a taxi where there are other people around, ensure that your call is not overheard by someone who could then later masquerade as your driver. Ask the cab firm what type of car your driver will arrive in and find out his name and call sign. Ensure that the firm informs the driver of your name and, when your driver arrives, this information can be verified. Insist on sitting in the back of the cab and do not discuss your personal details. If you are suspicious about the driver, ask him to drop you off at the nearest busy public place.

■ ■ ■ ■ ■ Personal Attack Alarms ■ ■ ■ ■ ■

Carrying a personal attack alarm is an extremely effective means of deterring an assailant. A street thug wants to pounce on his innocent victim and then escape without fuss or delay. The immediate deafening shriek that a personal attack alarm emits will also act to stun an assailant momentarily in much the same way that hitting your fingernail with a hammer will momentarily stun you.

There are several types of attack alarms available and one that I would particularly recommend is the **Personal Defender Alarm** supplied by Summit Accessories Ltd. This product, which sells for about £20, is available from all good DIY and car accessory shops or, in cases of difficulty, can be supplied direct by Summit.

The alarm itself, weighing just over three ounces, has been designed to be used in many different situations. For example, it can be worn round the waist using the supplied waist clip, or its bracket can be fitted to the car by means of the supplied self-adhesive pads, enabling you to remove the alarm when you leave the car and carry it with you. By pulling the cord, the alarm emits a deafening 130-decibel piezo siren that is designed to see off all but the most persistent of thugs. It can also be used to secure doors, giving advance warning of intruders and can be linked to your handbag or briefcase to combat the sneak thief.

I have included Summit's address and telephone number in the section **Useful Addresses** at the end of this book.

■ ■ ■ ■ ■ ■ Home Security ■ ■ ■ ■ ■ ■

Burglary is one of the most common crimes. Its effects on the victim can be devastating. But what exactly can we do to protect our homes against it? The fact is that there is a lot that we can do. Many burglaries are opportunistic. Many are preventable. You can substantially decrease the chances of your home being burgled by taking some pretty basic security precautions. Later in this section, I will deal with locks for the doors – but please remember to change all locks when you move into a new home and whenever you lose your keys, and *never* give your keys to workmen, as copies can easily be made.

First, let us look at some statistics concerning burglaries. In 1992 there were almost 700,000 domestic burglaries in this country. Only about 20 per cent of these were committed by professional criminals. In roughly 30 per cent of cases the burglar didn't even have to force his way in as either doors or windows were left open. Over 65 per cent of unlawful entries were made through windows and 80 per cent of burglaries occurred when the property was empty.

Most homes are broken into during the day. Contrary to common belief, violence during a burglary is rare. If the burglar is detected, his objective is to escape, preferably without being seen or being confronted by the occupier.

Burglars, like most other criminals, like to pick easy targets. The chances are that if they have to spend a lot of time, make a lot of noise or risk being seen, they will not bother. Burglars dislike locked windows and security deadlocks because to get past them usually means creating noise and spending more time in attempting to gain entry. If a window is secured with a window lock then, even after breaking the glass, the burglar won't be able to open it, the only option being for him to climb in through the broken glass. The same deterrent also applies to security deadlocks fitted to doors. These will only open with a key, so even if the burglar does manage to gain entry via the window, he will have to leave by the same method, as he will be unable to open the door from the inside.

These are all pretty simple precautions and are relatively inexpensive to fit. For considerably less than £100, you will be able to secure all windows and doors with good quality security locks, making your home more secure – and it will also give you greater peace of mind.

The drawing on pages 108–9 illustrates a typical house and the measures that can be taken to help secure it. Ensure that all security fittings are fitted with strong bolts or screws, so that they cannot be wrenched out easily.

Flats too can be vulnerable to burglaries. Many purpose-built blocks of flats are surrounded by either garden areas or open space. Those on the ground floor are more vulnerable than others, as access can be gained by the front, rear or side. Upper-storey flats can usually only be accessed by their front doors or adjoining windows. As a precaution, you should still keep the windows locked, as the intruder could find a ladder by which he could enter your flat. In converted flats, the dwellings in the basement and ground floor are potentially more vulnerable than those on the upper floors.

Most areas of the country operate a **Neighbourhood Watch** scheme. Since the very first scheme which started in Mollington, Cheshire in 1982, Neighbourhood Watch is now a well established part of crime prevention. They have succeeded in reducing crime in many areas of the country as well as providing a useful means of co-ordination and co-operation between the police and the community.

There are three main elements to Neighbourhood Watch: vigilance, security and property marking. Local schemes are operated by local members of the community concerned. Advice is always on hand from the local police who would, almost certainly, have been involved in the setting up of the scheme and often attend the local meetings in order to provide information and guidance.

Neighbourhood Watch-type schemes are not limited to residential neighbourhoods. Business Watch schemes can prove to be very effective in

a. Burglar alarms act as a visible deterrent to burglars. Check that the system you buy meets British Standard 4737 if the alarm is being professionally installed, or 6707 if it is a DIY type.

b. Fit good-quality security locks to front and rear external doors. Many unauthorized entries are made through rear (and side) doors, as there is often less risk of being seen. Fit a deadlock which meets British Standard 3621 and has a British Standard Kitemark. A deadlock can be opened only with a key, so even if a burglar smashes a window, he cannot reach through to open the door. Neither will he be able to carry your property out through the door. Fitting two locks, spaced apart, on a door will help spread the load on both the door and the frame and will appear more impregnable from the outside.

c. Fit a good-quality security chain and 'spy hole' viewer to the front (or main) door.

d. Ensure window locks are also fitted to windows on upper floors, particularly if there is a porch attached to the front door, as the roof of the porch makes these windows more vulnerable. These windows can also be accessed by climbing drainpipes.

e. Patio doors should be fitted with special locks, both top and bottom. Anti-lift devices are also available to stop the doors being lifted off their rails.

f. Louvre windows are particularly vulnerable, because the slats are easily removed from the frame. To increase security, the glass slats can be glued using an epoxy resin. There are also special louvre window locks that can be fitted.

g. Lights controlled by timer switches will switch your lights on and off at pre-set times to give the impression that the house is occupied. Lights are also available that switch themselves on and off intermittently, or whenever a noise is detected.

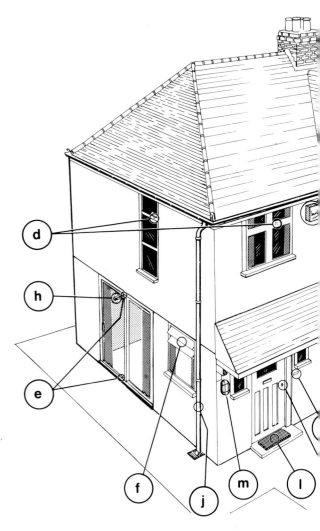

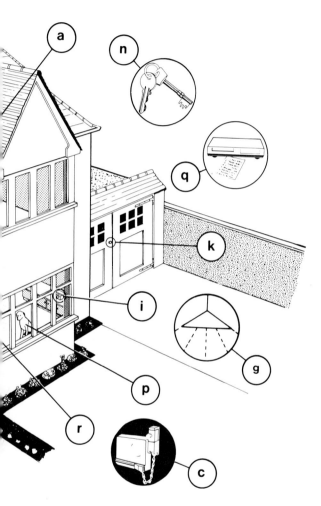

h. Infra-red detectors can be fitted to rooms to detect movement. These are connected to the main alarm system.

i. When you are out, leave a light on, and perhaps a radio playing.

j. Use anti-climb paint on drainpipes, but not as a substitute for window locks on the upper floors.

k. Never leave a garage (or garden shed) unlocked, especially if it has a connecting door attached to the house, as a burglar can use the garage to hide while he is forcing an inner door. Garages and sheds also contain some very useful tools for the burglar to use to gain entry into your house and ladders can be used to access upper windows.

l. Never hide a spare key under a door mat or in some other convenient hiding place. A burglar could quite easily find it. He will probably know where to look.

m. Security lighting can be fitted to the perimeter of the house and can be activated by movement. It can also be used in a static state so that the lighting is controlled by a switch. Ensure that the porch and other doors are lit to make the intruder visible.

n. Do not put your name or address on your keys in case you lose them or they are stolen, and, in these circumstances, remember to change all locks as soon as possible.

o. Don't allow your doorbell to advertise that you are female and on your own.

p. A dog is a good deterrent if it barks when strangers approach or when it hears a noise. You can also buy security devices containing a recording of a barking dog that is activated by noise. In any event, displaying a 'Beware of the dog' sign can act as a deterrent.

q. Keep a list of your more valuable items together with their serial numbers. Consider marking them with a security marking pen.

r. Always draw your curtains at night.

areas such as trading estates and the Watch schemes even extend to farms and harbours.

I would highly recommend you joining one of these schemes and further information can be obtained from the Crime Prevention Officer at your local police station. In addition, you can always discuss general security matters with the Crime Prevention Officer. They can often give you the details of local security firms and locksmiths. They may also be able to visit your home to discuss with you how you can increase your security generally.

■ ■ ■ Home Security While You Are Away ■ ■ ■

As 80 per cent of burglaries occur when the property is empty, it is important to take additional precautions when you are away from home, particularly for any length of time. The following list will assist you to prevent burglaries in these circumstances:

■ Never publicize your absence when you are away from home, particularly when you are away on holiday.
■ Inform your local police of the dates you intend to leave and return.
■ Ask a friend or neighbour to keep an eye on the house when you are away on holiday.
■ Arrange for someone to remove the mail and any papers from the mat.
■ Ask a friend or neighbour to adjust the curtains regularly, to remove any leaves that have fallen and to mow the lawn, so as to give the impression that the house is being lived in.
■ Cancel the milk and any newspapers, but never leave a note in the milk bottle to notify the milkman of your absence.

> '*I contacted my local police station and asked to speak to the Crime Prevention Officer. He was ever so helpful. He called round and reviewed my home security. My home is now much more secure and I feel a lot safer.*'

Some insurance companies offer reduced premiums to householders who have fitted burglar alarms and security locks. However, they might insist on a particular type or specification.

■ ■ ■ ■ Malicious Telephone Callers ■ ■ ■ ■

Malicious or other nuisance telephone calls can be particularly distressing, not just because of the nature of the call, but also because the victim is usually unaware of the caller's identity, or from where he is calling. The caller may know you or he may simply have picked your telephone number from the directory or even dialled it at random. Malicious calls can be indecent, menacing, or simply very annoying. These calls may also be a criminal offence under Section 43 of the Telecommunications Act, 1984.

As a precaution, it is wise not to place your first name in the telephone directory, and women should never be listed as Miss, Mrs or even Ms. Your initials should suffice. Don't recite your name and telephone number when you answer the phone, simply say 'Hello'. If a stranger calls, never disclose information about yourself or say that you are alone.

Similarly, if you have a telephone answering machine, don't record your name and number in your opening message or say that you are out, or on holiday. Your message should state simply that you can't answer the phone in person at the moment.

If a caller asks you for your name or number, reply by asking who, or what number, is required, and then only tell the caller whether they are correct or not. Do not give your telephone number to callers or answer any questions over the telephone unless you know and trust the caller. Ensure that other members of your household also follow this procedure.

If you do receive a nuisance call, try not to show your annoyance to the caller, or to react to the call in any way, or engage in conversation, as this could be just the reaction that the caller wants. Simply put the receiver down beside the phone and ignore it for a few minutes before replacing it. Alternatively, you could temporarily unplug your telephone from the socket. If the phone rings again, don't say anything when answering. A genuine caller will speak first, whereas a malicious caller will almost certainly just hang up. Do not be tempted to blow a whistle down the telephone as this could excite the caller to continue to pester you.

Always report persistent cases to British Telecom or, if you feel particularly threatened, to the police.

To help conquer this problem, British Telecom have established a Malicious Calls Bureau, where a team of specially trained BT staff work in conjunction with the police to combat these nuisance calls. They have, at their disposal, a range of solutions, such as *call tracing* by which almost all malicious calls can now be traced.

They could also offer you a *new telephone number*, in which case they recommend you keep it ex-directory, to prevent the offender from making further contact with you.

Another solution that BT offer is *call interception*, where all calls are intercepted by the operator who will only connect those callers who can correctly identify the recipient's name and number.

If you are ever on the receiving end of malicious calls and would like further advice, call British Telecom's Malicious Calls Advice Line FREE on 0800 666 700 where you will hear a recorded message advising you how to deal with the problem and what to do if you need further assistance. Alternatively, dial 150 to speak personally to the Customer Service Advisors, who will offer you information about how BT can help you to combat this problem.

■ ■ ■ ■ ■ Men Can Help Too! ■ ■ ■ ■ ■

With just a little effort, men can also help by taking care not to frighten or otherwise alarm women, who may be nervous when they are out alone, especially at night or in deserted or enclosed areas. The following points would prove helpful to women:

- Do not sit too close to a woman on her own on a bus or a train.
- Do not stare at a woman, as your admiring looks could be mistaken and the woman could feel threatened by them.
- If you happen to be walking in the same direction as a woman alone, particularly on a deserted, unlit road, cross the road rather than walk behind her. This may reassure her that you are not following her.
- If you are with other males, do not pass comment on a woman, as she is not to know that your comments are just innocent 'boys' talk'.

You can also help women friends by offering them a lift or by walking them home. Remember, a little inconvenience on your part can make a woman feel much safer. Remember too that a woman has the right to say '*No*' and mean it. You must always respect her right to refuse whatever she doesn't want, no matter what the circumstances.

> '*He came and sat next to me on the train. The remainder of the carriage was empty. He kept trying to start a conversation with me. He was probably a decent chap who only wanted a chat to break the boredom of the journey. I was afraid and on edge for the rest of the journey. I even thought he was going to follow me off the train. Unfortunately these days, you just don't know who you can trust.*'

■ ■ ■ ■ ■ Alcohol and Drugs ■ ■ ■ ■ ■

Alcohol and drugs are significant factors in violence generally. Around half of all violent crimes are committed by people who have either been drinking alcohol or taking drugs. The term 'violent crime', of course, includes the perpetrating of any kind of violence by one person on another and should not be taken to refer only to crimes such as robbery and mugging. In addition, many rows and relationship breakdowns are caused by these substances. It would be wise, therefore, to avoid such substances altogether at times of anger and anxiety, particularly when you consider there is a possibility that you may discharge your anger through the use of violence.

Alcohol and drugs can also affect your judgement of situations and other people.

> '*I really trusted him – he seemed such a decent guy. I know I was drunk at the time and I didn't have a care in the world. I wish now that I hadn't had so many drinks.*'

■ ■ ■ ■ ■ Domestic Violence ■ ■ ■ ■ ■

Domestic violence is as much a crime as any other type of violence. Nobody has the right to assault you physically, sexually or emotionally. Violence within the home is little different to violence on the street, although many, particularly the perpetrators, often see it differently. Just because two people decide to live together, whether as man and wife or otherwise, clearly doesn't give one party the right to inflict violence on the other. However, despite the wrongs of this subject, violence in the home is an unfortunate fact of everyday life. But just what options does the victim have when faced with violence at the hands of their co-habitee?

In researching this subject, I spoke to Mrs Sonia Abrahamson, who is the senior matrimonial law executive of A. D. Abrahamson & Co., part of Edwards Abrams Doherty, solicitors in Liverpool. She specializes in dealing with domestic violence, more often referred to as 'wife battering', although, as she pointed out to me, she also has to deal with husbands who have been on the receiving end of violence from their wives.

I asked her what advice she would give to a wife or female co-habitee who suffers from violence at the hands of her male partner. First, she identified that approximately 40 per cent of all domestic violence cases are alcohol-related, 5 per cent are associated with drugs, and a further 15 per cent are due to financial difficulties. The remainder, she puts down to general unhappiness within the relationship, with violence being the chosen way of expressing dissatisfaction.

Sonia's view is that if violence persists within a relationship then the only real solution is to end the association, even though she accepts that it often takes more strength to break a relationship than it does to persevere with it. She added that some victims prefer to remain with a violent partner rather than face life alone.

When the violence within the relationship is very severe, it is often necessary to seek an emergency injunction to remove the violent party from the home and to keep them from contacting the innocent partner. Sonia emphasized that whenever her firm is contacted with a view to obtaining such an injunction, they **always** make time to see the client straight away and they operate an emergency service specifically designed for this purpose.

Often, victims of domestic violence can be deterred by the cost of court proceedings but, as Sonia explained, legal aid could be available to help with legal costs, so expense should not prevent victims seeking expert help. She explained that legal aid usually takes more than a week to be approved, and even in urgent cases as long as a few days. However, where the situation is extremely serious, emergency legal aid can be obtained by the solicitor. The client can then be taken before a judge and an injunction can be obtained there and then on an ex-parte basis, which means that the complainant's case is heard without reference to or representation by the other party. This course of action is only used in cases of extreme violence to the adult and in some cases to the children. A full court hearing is then arranged, usually seven days later, when the court has the opportunity to hear both sides. In the meantime, the complainant, and the children, have the immediate protection of the court.

Another matter that often deters women from obtaining an injunction against a violent partner is that, despite the severity of the violence, the woman does not want to involve the police. However, this is a totally separate matter altogether and there is no reason at all why the police need to be involved, if the woman does not want them to be.

While I was in her office, a woman came in to seek her assistance. She had been badly assaulted by her spouse who had threatened to kill her. Sonia dealt with the woman immediately and within two hours she had prepared all the necessary papers, briefed a barrister (who in this instance was her daughter Sharon!) and had made all the arrangements necessary to present the case to a judge later that day. Sonia told me afterwards that she would expect to have the injunction granted within the next hour – making a total of three hours from start to end. After an injunction is granted, a process server will serve it on the partner, and the partner is required to vacate the home immediately, although the court can overturn its decision if it later transpires that the injunction was wrongly obtained. In many cases, Sonia attends court personally with her clients as this gives them a greater sense of security and continuity.

Children, too, are a concern where violence exists within the home. Many injunctions are obtained where there is concern for the children, and a residence order (previously known as custody) can be procured so that the children remain with the party who would best serve their interests.

Sonia readily admits that when she first became involved in her particular speciality she found her work emotionally involving. She said that she was appalled to discover how human beings could be so cruel in every way to each other, but when she sees a woman, who has previously sobbed her heart out in front of her, start to smile and tell her that she feels better already, it proves that her work is tremendously worthwhile. She told me that perhaps the worst kind of wife battering goes on behind the net curtains of the more respectable areas. In those cases, women are more frightened of seeking help due to the embarrassment of what the neighbours might think, but eventually they are left with no other option other than to seek urgent expert help.

The greatest recognition Mrs Abrahamson receives is the many letters of thanks and appreciation from her clients and their children, which she affixes to her office wall.*

*During my discussion with Mrs Abrahamson, she did not refer to any of her clients by name or disclose any other information about them which could identify them in any way.

'I stood for it for far too long. He used to beat me regularly, particularly when he was drunk. He would always apologize and swear he would never hit me again. I suppose deep down I really knew he would never change. One day he beat me so badly that I was detained in hospital for several days. That was the turning point as far as I was concerned. I saw a solicitor and she got an injunction preventing him from even contacting me. My self-respect has now returned and I am so much happier in myself. I will never know why I allowed him to beat me for so long.'

■ ■ ■ ■ Self Defence and the Law ■ ■ ■ ■

Before learning the techniques taught in this book, or considering joining any self-defence classes, it is important to understand how self defence relates to the law, to ensure that you will not be breaking the law yourself when faced with a dangerous or potentially dangerous situation.

Section 3 of the Criminal Law Act 1967 provides the authority for the use of 'reasonable force' in circumstances such as when defending yourself or others who are under attack, or the prevention of crime. What constitutes reasonable force does, of course, depend on the circumstances, and careful thought needs to be given to assess the severity of the situation as the law only permits you to respond accordingly.

While it is universally recognized that we all have a right to defend ourselves, this right has to be considered and qualified within the context of the law.

'Reasonable force' is in many cases extremely difficult to judge. What might seem reasonable to one person might be considered as wholly unacceptable to another.

When faced with a situation, you should first ask yourself whether a physical response is necessary. For example, it would be totally wrong for you to respond physically to verbal insults, no matter how hurtful they might be. A physical response should only be considered when there is a real possibility of an attack and even then your response should only be appropriate to the situation you are facing.

Clearly, if your response to an over-zealous and persistent vagrant was to break his arm simply because he stretched out towards you in a begging motion, you would more than likely face prosecution. And quite right too. However, should you cause a similar fate to a knife-wielding attacker who had demanded money from you, you could well be justified, as this could constitute a bonafide action of self-defence. It is worth noting that many of the techniques taught in this book allow you to control the amount of force that you apply, thereby allowing you to control the situation with which you are faced.

■ ■ ■ ■ Weapons and Self Defence ■ ■ ■ ■

When considering the law, one also needs to have regard to weapons. Weapons divide into two categories.

Class 1 weapons are best described as weapons which are offensive in themselves and include such things as batons, flick-knives and knuckledusters, and are unlawful to possess. **You are forbidden by law to carry such weapons for any reason, including self defence.** A prosecution could well result if a person is found with them.

Class 2 weapons are not actually designed as weapons at all, but can be so used. They consist of virtually anything – for example bottles, hat pins, aerosols and walking sticks. With these, intent has to be shown in order to secure a conviction in court.

Under no circumstances is a person entitled to

carry any object with the intention of using it as a weapon.

You may recall the case of Mr Eric Butler, a fifty-six-year-old man who received a twenty-eight-day suspended prison sentence and a £200 fine for using a sword stick to stab a drunken youth who had attacked him on a crowded train. This sentence was given, despite the judge describing Mr Butler at his trial as being 'of excellent character'. While many people would find this sentence alarming and would be pleased that natural justice was served by an older man defending himself against a drunken youth who had just attacked him – even if he did use a weapon to do so – the law obviously cannot condone or disregard this sort of conduct, otherwise a dangerous precedent could be set which could encourage other people to carry weapons, which would inevitably lead to more serious incidents.

If you do have cause to use anything as a weapon in self defence, it must only be used as a last resort and after having given due consideration to all of the circumstances facing you.

If you think that your life is seriously in danger, then defending yourself with a weapon is better than suffering serious injury. But be warned, reasonableness is always a subjective matter, and what appears to be reasonable in the heat of the moment, may not seem so later in a court room.

Many everyday items can be used as weapons for self-defence purposes. I have described above just some of these items. Let us now consider some items that might be found in a woman's handbag, and how such everyday items can be used for self-defence.

Hairbrush or Comb

These items can be used to scratch or rake at exposed skin. The face, particularly around the eyes, nose and mouth are particularly painful targets to aim for.

Keys

Keys can be used to gouge your assailant's face. Again, the areas around the eyes, nose and mouth are the best targets to aim for. They can also be laced through your fingers and used when striking.

Perfume or breath spray

These items can be squirted into your assailant's eyes. As a minimum, this will have the effect of causing them to smart and water, which will give you sufficient time to make your escape.

Pen or make-up brush

These can be used to poke your assailant in the eyes.

Coins

These can be laced between your fingers and used to strike your assailant in or across the face.

Handbag

The handbag itself is often filled with heavy objects and can be used to smash into your assailant's face, stomach or groin.

Briefcase

A briefcase can be used to smash into an assailant in just the same way as a handbag.

Men could well have some of the above items in their pockets and they can be used in just the same way as described above.

Additionally, consider how many other items that you could be carrying can be used as a weapon to defend yourself. An umbrella can be used to jab the assailant in his eyes or groin, or it can be used to hit him. A book's edge can be used to strike the assailant under his nose and a rolled up newspaper can be used to jab him either in the throat or under his nose.

Think about the possibilities of adapting other things that you could use as a weapon to defend yourself in the event of being attacked. Perhaps you are using a payphone: the phone itself can be used to strike the assailant. Or, maybe you are eating a sandwich: try smashing and rubbing it in his face to distract him before escaping. Or a drink: throw it at his face. Even a handful of stones found in the road can be used to blind an assailant momentarily, giving you valuable time to escape.

At home, consider what is at hand that can be thrown at an assailant – an iron or a kettle full of hot water, perhaps. The possibilities are endless. They are only limited by your ability to think quickly enough under pressure of this kind.

■ ■ ■ ■ ■ Coping After an Attack ■ ■ ■ ■ ■

No matter how proficient you become in self defence and no matter how careful you are, it is of course possible that you may still fall victim to an attack. With the help of this book, you will develop self-protection skills and the more proficient you become the more you will reduce the likelihood of being attacked. However, you cannot eliminate the risks altogether.

I feel, therefore, that, in order to provide you with a complete course on self defence, I must include a chapter which deals with the aftermath of an attack. In the event of either being a victim or a witness to a violent incident, the following information will prove useful.

Trauma

Many victims of a violent attack suffer intense trauma, sometimes for years after the attack has occurred and the physical signs have long disappeared. Regrettably, this can also have the effect of undermining that person's confidence. Unfortunately, this negative projection is directly opposite to the desired confident image that is so important.

A victim can, depending upon the nature of the assault, experience some or all of the following reactions:

- Fear and panic attacks, particularly when out alone.
- Recurring visions of the attack.
- Reluctance to return to the scene of the attack.
- Feelings of deep depression.
- Loss of interest in sex (particularly in cases of sexual assault).
- Anger due to the inability to recover stolen property.
- Insomnia.
- Nightmares.

- Delayed shock.
- Remorse due to inaction at the time of the attack.
- Anger with yourself and others – including those close to you.
- Asking 'why me – what did I do to deserve this?'

If the trauma is particularly severe and you find that your ability to cope with your feelings and your daily life is being inhibited, then you should consult your General Practitioner and ask to be referred to a therapist who is experienced in such matters. Alternatively, there are a number of organizations to which you can turn for help. A list of some of these organizations can be found in the section **Useful Addresses** on page 125.

Guilt

It is all too easy to 'freeze' in the face of an assault, rendering the victim incapable of fighting back. Some people translate this fear into guilt and consider that they were somehow to blame. Even those people who actively resist their assailant sometimes experience these feelings.

It is an unfortunate consequence of being the victim of a violent crime that even those who are there to help you often ask damaging questions, which can only add delay to the healing process. Questions such as 'Why did you wear that short skirt?' or 'Why did you let him into your home?' can be deeply distressing, even though they have been asked with the best of intentions.

The most important thing to remember is that *you are not to blame for being the victim of an assault.* Your attacker, and he alone, is the guilty party. Any attempt to blame you for your assailant's actions only attempts to provide an excuse for an inexcusable crime.

■ ■ ■ ■ Keeping Your Children Safe ■ ■ ■ ■

Children are particularly vulnerable to attack and it is really up to us as adults to protect and teach them how to look after themselves and to avoid danger. Much of what is contained in this book will prove invaluable to youngsters and this section looks specifically at the protection and safety of children.

It can be a difficult task in itself to alert your children to the dangers of the world, without having to worry about depriving them of their innocence, but it *can* be done without being alarmist.

Kidscape is an organization which exists to help protect children. They have developed a ten-point code to help parents protect their children. I have reproduced this code here with their kind permission:

1. **TO BE SAFE.** Teach children that everyone has rights, such as the right to breathe, which should not be taken away. Tell children that no one should take away their right to be safe.
2. **TO PROTECT THEIR OWN BODIES.** Children need to know that their body belongs to them, particularly the private parts covered by their swimsuits.
3. **TO SAY NO.** Tell children it's all right to say 'No' to anyone if that person tries to harm them. Most children are taught to listen to and obey adults and older people without question.
4. **TO GET HELP AGAINST BULLIES.** Bullies usually pick on younger children. Tell children to enlist the help of friends or say 'No' without fighting – and to tell an adult. Bullies are cowards and a firm, loud 'No' from a group of children with the threat of adult intervention often puts them off.

    In cases of real physical danger, children often have no choice but to surrender to the bully's demands. Sometimes children will fight and get hurt to protect a possession because of the fear of what will happen when they arrive home without it. *'My mum will kill me for letting the bullies take my bike. It cost a lot of money.'* Tell children that keeping themselves safe is the most important consideration.
5. **TO TELL.** Assure your children that no matter what happens, you will not be angry with them and that you want them to tell you of any incident. Children can also be very protective of parents and might not tell about a frightening occurrence because they are worried about your feelings.
6. **TO BE BELIEVED.** When children are told to go to an adult for help, they need to know they will be believed and supported. Although sometimes an immediate reaction is to say 'I told you so', this will not help the child to resolve the problem. It could also prevent the child from seeking help another time.

    This is especially true in the case of sexual assault, as children very rarely lie about it. If the child is not believed when he or she tells, the abuse may continue for years and result in suffering and guilt for the child.
7. **TO NOT KEEP SECRETS.** Teach children that some secrets should NEVER be kept, no matter if they promised not to tell. Child molesters known to the child often say that a kiss or touch is 'Our secret'. This confuses the child who has been taught always to keep secrets.
8. **TO REFUSE TOUCHES.** Explain to children that they can say 'Yes' or 'No' to touches or kisses from anyone, but that no one should ask them to keep touching a secret. Children sometimes do not want to be hugged or kissed, but that should be a matter of choice, not fear. They should not be forced to hug or kiss anyone.
9. **TO NOT TALK TO STRANGERS.** It is NEVER a good idea to talk to a stranger. Since most well-meaning adults or teenagers do not approach children who are by themselves (unless the child is obviously lost or in distress), teach children to ignore any such approach. Children do not have to be rude, they can pretend not to hear and quickly walk or run away. Tell children you will never be

angry with them for refusing to talk to strangers and that you want to know if a stranger talks to them.

10. **TO BREAK RULES.** Tell your children that they have your permission to break all rules to protect themselves and tell them you will always support them if they must break a rule to stay safe. For example, it is all right to run away, to yell and create a fuss, even to lie or kick to get away from danger.

Kidscape also offer the following advice to children:

■ Don't answer the door if you are at home on your own.
■ Don't tell anyone over the telephone that you are at home alone. Say that your mum will ring back, she's in the bath – or any other excuse you can think of.
■ Always tell your parents or whoever is taking care of you where you are going and how you can be contacted.
■ If you get lost, go to a shop or a place with lots of people and ask for help, or find a policeman or policewoman to ask.
■ Travel in a carriage of a train where there are other people.
■ When you're out on your own, keep far enough away from people you don't know so that you can't be grabbed and so you can run away.
■ Never play in deserted or dark places.
■ Carry enough money for your return trip home and never spend it on anything else.
■ Memorize your telephone number and address.
■ Know how to contact your parents or a neighbour.

■ If you have no money, but need to ring home in an emergency, dial 100 and ask the operator to place a reverse-charge call.
■ Learn how to make an emergency telephone call:
1. Dial 999 and the operator will say, 'Emergency, which service?'
2. You will then ask for the emergency service that you require – typically the police, fire or ambulance service.
3. The operator will then put you through to the required emergency service, who will then deal with your call and help you. Try to keep calm and speak clearly when you are connected and listen carefully to what is being said to you.

The operator will automatically know the number of the telephone that you are using to make the call, although in some areas (where there is no digital exchange), you could also be asked for this number. If you don't know, or you can't read the number clearly, tell the operator. This process sounds as though it would take a long time, but it usually happens very quickly.
■ Always get an adult to make an emergency telephone call, if possible. NO ONE should ever make one unless there is a real emergency.

Kidscape produce a number of useful guides dealing with different aspects of safety and protection for children, including bullying and sexual abuse. They also provide information guides for teachers and trainers.

*For further information about protection for children, contact Kidscape. Their details are listed in the section **Useful Addresses** on page 125.*

■ ■ ■ Further Self-Defence Training ■ ■ ■

After having studied the techniques taught in this book, you may wish to further your self-defence training. As with anything, it is practice that makes perfect and this is very much the case with self defence.

The British Self Defence Governing Body

(BSDGB) maintains a list of qualified instructors throughout the country. The BSDGB also organizes its own self-defence courses. As Chief Instructor of the BSDGB, I teach at many of them. The BSDGB can be contacted at :

The British Self Defence Governing Body
Price Street Business Centre
Price Street
Birkenhead
Merseyside
L41 4JQ

In addition to self defence, there are many martial arts classes available throughout the country. It is my view, and that of other senior self-defence teachers, that learning a martial art in order to learn self defence takes a very long time for you to become reasonably proficient. However, if you are interested in learning that particular martial art anyway, then the additional benefits in terms of learning self-defence skills can be very useful.

That is not to say that I am against the martial arts. Far from it. In fact, I have studied them since the late 1960s and have been teaching the subject since the late 1970s. I was awarded my first black belt in 1974. During this period, I have competed, taught and refereed both in this country and abroad on a number of occasions. I was appointed an examiner in 1980, and a senior referee in 1985, positions I held for several years.

The martial arts are a wonderful and enjoyable activity to pursue and offer a great deal to those involved with them. In self-defence terms, they can be extremely useful, particularly if you have been studying them for some time.

However, it is important to understand that martial arts are taught and practised in 'controlled' situations and martial arts championships are fought under strict contest rules, adjudicated by a referee. In a real-life self-defence situation there are no rules and there is no referee to step in when things go too far. Regrettably, one only has to read the newspapers to be reminded of that.

As you will see from the following section, there are many martial arts systems – some you may have heard of, such as *karate*, *judo* or *aikido* – as well as many that you may not have heard of, such as *taiho-jutsu*, *tang-soo-do* and *capoeira*. It is not only important to understand which combat systems work well for self-defence purposes, but more importantly which particular techniques in those systems are the best ones suited for this purpose.

The self-defence system taught in this book is of an eclectic nature, in that I have selected, from many systems, only those techniques that constitute effective self defence for people without other forms of combat experience. In addition, there is a lot of advice about the psychology of self defence, including tips about how to avoid potentially violent situations and how to de-escalate them should they occur.

■ ■ ■ ■ ■ Martial Arts Systems ■ ■ ■ ■ ■

Self defence is often associated with the martial arts and to a large extent they are inextricably linked. In this book, I have selected an amalgam of defences based largely upon a variety of martial arts systems and styles.

For those readers who are interested, this section explores the various forms and styles of the martial arts, from the popular ones to those that are extremely rare. As you will see from the following information, many of the arts have a fascinating history and are steeped in mystery and tradition, going far beyond just a fighting system.

Aikido, 'the way of spiritual harmony with energy', is a Japanese martial art, founded by the late master Morihei Ueshiba in the early 1930s. Ueshiba was a deeply religious man, who had, from an early age, studied many styles of *ju-jutsu*, but it was mainly from the ancient thirteenth-century style of *daito-ryu* that his inspiration led to the development of *aikido*. The art incorporates throws, hold downs, joint-leverage techniques and weapons training. Today, there are two main styles of *aikido* – *Ueshiba* and *Tomiki* (named after its founder Kenji Tomiki who was also a famous judo exponent), the latter style including a competitive element.

Arnis´de mano, 'harness of the hand', is a stick fighting art from the Philippines using thirty-inch rattan canes. It is similar in many respects to *escrima* (see below). This art also incorporates kicks, strikes, joint-locking and throwing techniques.

Capoeira is an African martial art brought to Brazil by slaves from Angola and is usually performed to music. The combination of martial art techniques with dance and acrobatic movements was originally intended to disguise the fighting art and to prevent the slaves' captors from realizing that their slaves were practising a system of combat.

Escrima is a Philippine martial art using the staff as well as the empty hand for combat. Together with its sister arts, *arnis de mano* and *kali*, it was kept secret by the Filipinos until it first received Western attention in the early sixteenth century, when the Spanish invaded the Philippines and proscribed all forms of martial arts training. However, despite this, the Filipinos disguised their art and practised it as stage plays, known as 'moro-moro', which often concluded with a mock battle fought with various types of blade. It is often argued, although wrongly, that it was the Spanish who brought *escrima* to the Philippines.

Hapkido, 'the way of co-ordinated power', is a Korean martial art consisting of punching, kicking, joint-locking and throwing techniques. Although not prominent in this country, *Hapkido* has been adopted by several police forces in the United States, due largely to the wide selection and application of its techniques.

Hsing-i chuan, 'form of mind', is a Chinese martial art, founded by Yu Fei, a Chinese general who had distinguished himself in battle against the Kin tribes during a period dating back to the tenth or eleventh century. Its techniques are derived from the movements of twelve animals: the bear, cock, dragon, eagle, falcon, hawk, horse, monkey, snake, swallow, tiger and turtle. These animal-type movements are combined with the five basic actions of the art – crossing, crushing, drilling, splitting and pounding. These movements, together with special foot movements, are used to strike an adversary and evade his attacks.

Iaido, 'the way of drawing', is a Japanese martial art, dating back to the mid sixteenth century, which developed from sword fighting techniques known as *iaijutsu*. Its aim was to draw the sword and kill the enemy in one single movement, *before* the enemy had the chance to draw his own sword. It is practised standing, sitting, kneeling and lying down. *Iaido* is closely linked to *kendo* (see page 121).

Jodo, 'the way of the staff', is a modern-day Japanese martial art using a short staff, about 125 centimetres in length, called the *jo*. It is distinguishable from the long staff, the *bo*, which is about twice its length. Its forerunner, *jo-jutsu*, was devised during the seventeenth century by Muso Gonnosuke, who realized that the previously deployed *bo* was not sufficient to deal with weapons like the sword. Like *iaido*, *jodo* is closely associated with *kendo*.

Judo, 'the way of gentleness', is derived from the ancient art of *ju-jutsu*. It was founded by the late Dr Jigoro Kano, who was originally a student of *ju-jutsu*, having studied several of its styles. Kano was a brilliant man who spoke excellent English. He was the headmaster of two eminent Japanese high schools. He was also responsible for creating the Japanese Olympic Committee. In order for Kano to facilitate the large-scale teaching of his newly created art, he established the world famous Kodokan judo centre in Tokyo in 1882, which served as *judo*'s world headquarters. *Judo* consists of throwing, grappling, strangling, choking and joint-locking techniques and its aim is to defeat the opponent by either throwing him forcefully onto his back, immobilizing him on the ground for thirty seconds or securing a submission from an armlock or a strangulation technique. *Judo* is scientific in the way it uses the laws of mechanics to generate spectacular throwing techniques, which are usually performed against the opponent's joints, such as the hip, shoulder or ankle, as joints generally are the weaker parts of the body. *Judo*'s remarkable armlocking and strangulation techniques are further examples of how *judoka* (practitioners) can defeat an opponent without having to employ a great amount of physical strength. *Judo* made its debut in 1964 when it was admitted as an Olympic sport at the Tokyo Games, some twenty-six years after Kano's death. Kano also originated the grading system of *Kyu* (pupil) and *Dan* (master) grades which are awarded to practitioners to denote the standard they have achieved in the art, and this grading system is now universally accepted throughout the world of modern martial arts. The *Dan* grades are usually symbolized by the wearing of a black belt while the *Kyu* grades wear differently coloured belts depending on the level achieved. However, the coloured-belt *Kyu* system is a Western innovation and is not used in Japan.

Ju-jutsu, 'techniques of gentleness', is an ancient Japanese martial art consisting of many styles and containing an extremely wide variety of skills, including grappling, striking, joint locking, throwing and weapons training techniques. The origins of *ju-jutsu* can be traced back to the seventh century and since that time its techniques have been elaborated and combined with others from both the Chinese combat styles as well as from the fighting techniques used by the Okinawan peasants. *Ju-jutsu* was developed, at least initially, to assist the largely unarmed warriors to defend themselves against their armed enemies. A Japanese law passed in the 1870s forbade the *Samurai* to carry their swords and this helped further to popularize the study of this art, as the newly unarmed *Samurai* needed to learn alternative methods of defence and combat. Although *ju-jutsu* is still widely practised in Britain, its popularity has largely been overtaken by other arts, particularly *judo* and *karate*.

Kali is another martial art from the Philippines and is similar to *arnis de mano* (see page 120).

Karate, 'art of the empty hand', is a popular martial art practised worldwide and consists of many forms or styles developed mainly in Japan, Korea and Okinawa. However, *karate* first came about during the sixteenth century when Okinawa was occupied by the Chinese, who forbade the inhabitants from carrying weapons of any kind. In order to defend themselves against the armed and invading soldiers, the peasants secretly devised and practised a means of combat which proved to be largely successful. Modern-day *karate* was first introduced by Funakoshi Gichin in 1922, when he staged exhibitions and tournaments to show this

art to the Japanese public. Because of the huge interest he created, he opened his own school and called it Shotokan. 'Shoto' was his nickname and 'kan' means school. Shotokan *karate* is the most widely taught style in the West. Other forms of *karate* include *goju-ryu*, *wado-ryu* and *shukokai*. *Karate* consists almost entirely of striking, kicking and blocking skills, although some styles also incorporate other techniques.

Kendo, 'the way of the sword', is a Japanese art using *shinai* (bamboo swords) and *dogu* (body armour). The *dogu* includes a face mask with metal grills, known as the *men*, and a hard breastplate traditionally made from lacquered bamboo, called the *do*. This art was originally known as *kenjutsu* and was developed initially by the Japanese *Bushi* and then further by the *Samurai* from the thirteenth century onwards. However, with the advent of modern weaponry and the supremacy of firearms, the use of the sword in warfare became almost obsolete. *Kenjutsu* was proscribed in the 1870s when the *Samurai* were forbidden to carry swords. In 1900, *kenjutsu* was transformed into the martial art we now know as *kendo* by Sakakibara Kenkichi. At that time it was intended, in particular, for the physical and the mental training of the young. The actual name of *kendo* was invented in that same year by Abe Tate, because he considered the term *kenjutsu* to be too warlike.

Kung-fu, 'human effort', is the frequently used term which covers a whole range of Chinese arts. It is closely related to the Zen philosophy and its creation can be traced back to the monks of the Shaolin Temple. *Kung-fu* consists of many different styles, some of them using weapons in their training. *Kung-fu* is much more than a fighting art. It is an intimate study and understanding of physical culture, theatre, dance, medicine, religion, history, legend and tradition as well as combat itself. To achieve a thorough understanding of *kung-fu*, one needs to dedicate a lifetime to studying the art, together with a comprehensive insight into Chinese history, traditions, life and customs. Probably the most significant religious influence on the Chinese martial arts was the arrival, around the fifth century, of a Buddhist teacher from India called Bodhidharma. He travelled from India to the Shaolin Temple in China where, initially, he was refused admission. He then retreated to a cave where he sat in meditation for nine years. Legend has it that, in order to prevent himself from falling asleep, he cut off his eyelids and that his lengthy period of meditation actually bored a hole in the mountain. In another tale we are told that his years of meditation caused his legs to fall off, which is why the Bodhidharma dolls on sale in Japan today are made with a round base and no legs. He was eventually admitted to the Temple where he created the Chan Buddhist sect, which was called Zen when it was later introduced to Japan. Bodhidharma is said to have created a system of unarmed combat, based upon Indian principles of fighting, although this contention has been disputed. In any event, it was this system that formed the basis for the majority of the Chinese martial arts.

Kyudo, 'the way of the bow', is the ancient Japanese art of archery. Prior to the Portuguese introducing firearms to Japan in the sixteenth century, this art, or *kyu-jutsu* as it was then known, was practised both for war and for hunting. However, the supremacy of firearms rendered *kyu-jutsu*, at least as a method of battle, almost obsolete. Bows that have been discovered have dated *kyu-jutsu* to the fifth century BC. Initially the use of the bow was kept to men on foot, but from around the twelfth century onwards it was used equally by horsemen. The bow, called the *yumi*, which is made of laminated bamboo, is asymmetrical and is approximately 2.20 metres long. This, together with the long arrow, the *ya*, makes up the armoury of the archer. Contrary to what might be expected, success in *kyudo* is not measured by hitting the centre of the target. It is considered that a successful *kyudoka* (practitioner) will fire his bow while being in the perfect frame of mind, which will preclude all desires of victory. It is thought that over half a million people in Japan currently practise *kyudo* and, in addition, many other countries also have *dojo* (training halls) where this ancient art is taught.

Ninjutsu is an ancient Japanese martial art, sometimes referred to as 'the art of invisibility' due to mythical tales of the *Ninja*'s extraordinary powers of being able to make themselves invisible and to perform amazing tasks such as walking on the ceiling. Early *Ninja* were skilled in many of the other arts around at the time, as well as being masters of disguise and illusion. These skills came about because they were usually involved in missions of spying, espionage and assassination and, accordingly, much about the *Ninja* was kept secret. *Ninja* were also used to help in the administration of justice. They were often secretly employed to spy and investigate the backgrounds of litigants to determine which ones were being truthful. The skills of pharmacy were also learned by *Ninja* to enable them to make poisons, antidotes and knockout drugs which were often administered in food or drink. It is probably because of the nature of the *Ninja*'s work and the fact that the punishment for revealing their secrets was death that little is known for certain about their origins. However, what is known, is that the *Ninja* became evident around the ninth century in the mountains around Kyoto in Japan and, by the beginning of the fifteenth century, they had become particularly prominent. The remainder of the *Ninja*'s scant history, as you might expect, is based largely on legend, tradition, conjecture and, to a lesser extent, fact. *The Art of War*, the celebrated definitive work written by General Sun Tzu around the year 500 BC, contained elements of the skills later attributed to the *Ninja*. This book is still read in military academies throughout the world and is credited as having been used as a reference by Mao Tse-tung and more recently it was read by General Schwarzkopf during the Gulf War. The book covers every aspect of military strategy from spy networks to tactics in the battlefield. It advises the warrior to appear suddenly, vanquish the enemy, then disappear into obscurity; and these skills were all prominent traits of the later *Ninja*. It could be said, therefore, that the art of *Ninjutsu* formally began somewhere around the publication of this book. In 1581, almost 4,000 *Ninja* were either killed or tortured by an army which outnumbered them by over ten to one. Those that managed to survive, passed on their art from father to son. The *Ninja*'s last known assignment was in 1673 during the Shimabara wars where they were used to fight against tens of thousands of Christians on the island of Kyushu. The techniques of *Ninjutsu* are varied and include striking, kicking, joint locking, throwing and weapons training skills.

Pakua, 'the eight hexagrams', is closely related to Chinese *kung-fu* and was created by a Taoist monk. Little else is known about its origins, other than it probably dates back to the eighteenth century. *Pakua* techniques consist of walking around an imaginary circle approximately 2.5 metres in diameter, then changing direction and retreating along the same circuit while deploying deflective arm movements. Single and double palm striking techniques also feature in this fighting style where evasion is a major feature of its strength.

Penchak-silat, 'lightning combat' (often abbreviated to *silat*) are styles of Indonesian and Malayan martial arts incorporating techniques similar to those found in *karate* and, in addition, containing weapons and groundwork fighting. In common with many other martial arts, spiritual power is an important characteristic in *silat* which is also steeped in ritual tradition. It is this tradition that tells us that students had to present to their master, referred to in *silat* as 'guru', a chicken whose blood would be smeared on the ground to symbolize the student's blood; a wrap of white material which could be used as a shroud to cover the student should he die while training; a knife to symbolize the extent of the student's sharpness and precision; and sufficient money to pay for new garments for the *guru*, should they be damaged during training. Although not common in this country, there are several hundred different styles of this ancient martial art system.

Ryukyu kobujutsu, 'the art of weapons', is a combat system utilizing Okinawan weaponry. Its history tells us that when the Okinawans were conquered and disarmed by the Japanese in 1609, they converted their farming implements into weapons in readiness for combat. Probably the most famous of these weapons are the *tonfa* and the *nunchaku*. Originally, the *tonfa* was the handle of the millstone used for grinding rice. Today the *tonfa*, or modified versions of it, are used by police forces around the world and can often be seen carried by police in American movies. The *tonfa* is a heavy wooden staff, between 45 and 60 centimetres long, with a handle fixed at right angles to the main section, three-quarters of the way along its length. In martial arts training, the *tonfa* is

often used in pairs. The *nunchaku*, whose origins come from rice and corn flails, are prominent in many *kung-fu* films. They consist of two equal length octagonal or cylindrical staffs, each of between 26 and 35 centimetres in length and are linked together by a cord or chain. They can be used as batons, where one piece is held and the other is swung at the enemy, or used to entrap or jab him. It can also be used as a vice by trapping the rival's limb between the two staffs. Other weapons used in this art include the *sai*, which is in the shape of a forked dagger; the *kama*, which is a kind of sickle with a long handle; the *ekku*, which is a wooden oar once used by the Okinawan fishermen against the Japanese *Samurai*; and the *timbe* and *rochin*, or tortoiseshell shield and short spear, which were generally used together. Other weapons used in *ryukyu kobujutsu* include the *tekko*, or knuckle-duster, which interestingly was also used as a weapon in the First World War and the *bo*, or long staff.

Savate, boxe Française, is a French boxing system which includes the use of the legs and feet in its art. Loosely, its techniques could be described as being similar to both boxing and *karate*. It was first put on the combat map by Michel Casseux in 1820 when he opened his first *salle*, or gym, in Paris. *Savate* is regarded as being very much on the periphery of the martial arts even though it adopts a grading system similar to many of them. Rather than wearing different coloured belts to denote their proficiency as is the case with many of the traditional martial arts, *savate* students wear different coloured gloves to indicate the grade that they have achieved.

Shorinji kempo, 'Boxing of the Shaolin Temple', is registered in Japan not as a martial art, but as a religion. It was established by Doshin So, just before the Second World War and can be widely described as a combination of *ju-jutsu*, *karate* and *aikido*. Being a religion, although its combat methods are both fearsome and well respected in the martial arts world, it has temples rather than training halls and the clothing worn is similar to the white *karate* uniform, although traditionalists sometimes wear the ceremonial monk's robe to signify the art's deeply religious foundation. Unlike many of the martial arts where one starts and ends a training session with a bow, in *shorinji kempo*, the greeting is made by placing the hands together, with the fingers spread, and held in front of the face. Zen meditation is also an important part of the philosophy of this art.

Sumo, the art of Japanese 'wrestling', is famous for its giant combatants, many weighing considerably more than 200 kilos. According to legend, its origins go back to a contest between two *Kami* (spirits) who fought for the possession of Japan. There are no weight categories in *sumo* and, despite the huge mountains of body crashing into one another, it is not uncommon to see a fighter being defeated by a rival weighing only half of his own weight. Considering their size, *sumotori* (sumo wrestlers) are remarkably fit. In Japan, there is a minimum height and weight for *sumotori*. The very first *sumo* contests were very much different to those of today. They were interrelated with religion and were fought to conciliate the *Kami* and to bring about a good harvest. These contests were held in the presence of the Emperor. According to Shinto ritual (Shinto is the name of the ancestral religion of Japan) the contest area has to be purified and both contestants then cleanse the specially built clay ring by throwing salt around themselves, while moving around the area. The aim of *sumo* is for one fighter to throw or drive the other outside the circle; to throw the opponent to the ground or to make any part of his opponent's body, except for his feet, touch the ground.

Taekwondo, 'the way of the foot and fist', is often referred to as Korean *karate* and is notable for its wide range of spectacular kicking techniques and its emphasis on breaking methods, where students learn how to smash bricks, tiles and wood with their bare hands and feet. *Taekwondo* is included in the training of soldiers in the Korean army. Its origins date back to the sixth century where it was referred to as *taekyon*, a name that was retained until about ten years after the liberation of Korea in 1945 when the name *taekwondo* was created. *Taekwondo* was seen by millions of people worldwide when it was admitted as a demonstration event in the 1988 Olympic Games in Seoul, Korea.

Tai chi chuan, 'supreme ultimate fist', is probably the oldest of the martial arts, first practised in China some five thousand years ago. The techniques and exercises are performed in an unhurried meditative manner and are practised more for exercise and fitness than for combat. Medical studies have suggested that *tai chi* reduces tension, calms the mind, and promotes benefits for health generally.

Taiho-jutsu, 'techniques of arrest', is a martial art created by the Japanese police in 1947. The art is eclectic in its nature, carefully selecting its techniques from a wide variety of other martial arts systems. In Britain, its techniques form the basis of self-defence training for police recruits. The British Self Defence Governing Body also draws heavily on *taiho-jutsu* for its own syllabus.

Tang-soo-do, 'the art of the Chinese hand', is a Korean martial art system similar to both *taekwondo* and Japanese *karate*. It consists mainly of punching and kicking techniques and, like *taekwondo*, it is noted for its spectacular kicking methods.

Wushu, 'the art of war', was the name originally given to the multitude of combative Chinese martial arts styles. Many of its techniques are almost gymnastic in the way they are performed, which has an important bearing on the practitioner's fitness and general state of health. A wide range of *wushu* techniques often feature in Beijing opera. In the West, *wushu*'s diverse styles, thought to number about 500, are often referred to indiscriminately as *kung-fu*, although this term is more accurately used to describe all of the Chinese arts. In 1928, the Chinese authorities tried to unify these various styles and create just one 'master' system, but their attempts met much opposition and failed. The techniques in *wushu* are vast and, in addition to the unarmed styles, some rather bizarre classical weapons are used, such as steel whips and double-ended daggers.

■ ■ ■ ■ ■ ■ Useful Addresses ■ ■ ■ ■ ■ ■

A. D. Abrahamson & Co. are a firm of solicitors specializing in domestic violence. See pages 112–113 for further information.

They can be contacted at Regina House, 1 Victoria Street, Liverpool L2 5TL. Tel. 051-236 9587.

Age Concern is involved with work including crime prevention information for the elderly. They also produce some useful publications.

They can be contacted at Astral House, 1268 London Road, London SW16 4ER. Tel. 081-679 8000.

Alcohol Concern provides useful information and a range of publications dealing with problems associated with alcohol. They also have access to a national network of advice centres.

They can be contacted at 275 Gray's Inn Road, London WC1X 8QF. Tel. 071-833 3471.

British Self Defence Governing Body is involved with all aspects of self defence and personal safety.

They can be contacted at Price Street Business Centre, Price Street, Birkenhead, Merseyside L41 4JQ.

British Telecom's Malicious Calls Advice Line carries a pre-recorded message advising how to combat malicious and nuisance telephone calls. The message also contains other useful telephone numbers.

Telephone (free) 0800 666 700, or dial 150 to speak personally with a Customer Service Advisor.

Citizens Advice Bureaux can help you obtain legal advice as well as providing local contact numbers for help organizations.

Their local number can be found in your local telephone directory.

Crime Prevention Officers can provide useful advice on a wide range of security matters.

They can be contacted via your local police station.

Criminal Injuries Compensation Board provides financial compensation to certain victims of violent crime.

They can be contacted at Blythswood House, 200 West Regent Street, Glasgow G2 4SW. Tel. 041-221 0945.

Help the Aged provides some very useful security advice for the elderly.

They can be contacted at St James Walk, London EC1R 0BE. Tel. 071-250 3399.

Kidscape has information packs available to help protect children.

They can be contacted at 152 Buckingham Palace Road, London SW1W 9TR. Tel. 071-730 3300.

National Society for the Prevention of Cruelty to Children (NSPCC) provides help and advice for the protection of children.

Their local number can be found in your local telephone directory or they can be contacted at 67 Saffron Hill, London EC1N 8RS. Tel. 071-242 1626.

Neighbourhood Watch are schemes operated throughout the country whose aim is to improve the security of the local community. Business Watch schemes are also available in some areas for the business community. For further information about your local Neighbourhood or Business Watch scheme, contact the Crime Prevention Officer at your local police station.

Rape Crisis Centre is manned by female volunteers and offers advice and assistance to victims.

Their local telephone number can be found in your local telephone directory.

Standing Conference on Drug Abuse (SCODA) provides useful information and a range of publications dealing with problems associated with drug abuse. They also have access to a national network of advice centres.

They can be contacted at 1–4 Hatton Place, London EC1N 8ND. Tel. 071-430 2341.

Summit Accessories Ltd supplies the Personal Defender Alarm (see page 106 for details).

They can be contacted at Unit 6, Wates Way, Wildmere Industrial Estate, Banbury, Oxfordshire OX16 7TS. Tel. 0295-270770.

Victim Support Schemes offer help and information to victims of crime.

Their local telephone number can be found in your local telephone directory. Your local police station can also put you in touch.

Index